Key West

PARADISE FOUND

Key West

PARADISE FOUND

ELLEN T. WHITE

Missy Janes, Photography

Pineapple Press

Palm Beach, Florida

Pineapple Press
An imprint of Globe Pequot, the trade division of The Rowman & Littlefield Publishing Group, Inc.
4501 Forbes Blvd., Ste. 200
Lanham, MD 20706
www.rowman.com

Distributed by NATIONAL BOOK NETWORK

British Library Cataloguing in Publication Information available

Library of Congress Cataloging-in-Publication Data

Names: White, Ellen T., author. | Janes, Missy (Photographer), photographer.
Title: Key West : paradise found / Ellen T. White ; photography by Missy Janes.
Description: Palm Beach, Florida : Pineapple Press, [2024]
Identifiers: LCCN 2024007442 (print) | LCCN 2024007443 (ebook) | ISBN 9781683343547 (cloth : acid-free paper) | ISBN 9781683343554 (epub)
Subjects: LCSH: Key West (Fla.)—History. | Key West (Fla.)—Social life and customs. | BISAC: TRAVEL / United States / South / South Atlantic (DC, DE, FL, GA, MD, NC, SC, VA, WV)
Classification: LCC F319.K4 W474 2024 (print) | LCC F319.K4 (ebook) | DDC 975.9/41—dc23/eng/20240221
LC record available at https://lccn.loc.gov/2024007442
LC ebook record available at https://lccn.loc.gov/2024007443

Printed in India

For departed heroes

José Martí, Jimmy Buffett, & Tom Hambright

and, always, for Paul

Contents

GETTY IMAGES

ANNETTE HOLMSTROM

Introduction

An Island Love Story

I first rolled into Key West at Christmas, 1999, along with my brother and sister-in-law. I'd never been to the island before but knew of its reputation, of course, as a tropical paradise. It was a feat to get to in those days. There were no direct flights, and you had to chart the path from Miami by plane or car. We chose to ramble down Overseas Highway. After more than three hours, we truly had the feeling that we'd reached a rock at the end of the world.

That Christmas we happily did what tourists in Key West do. We ate and drank ourselves senseless at the popular watering holes. We spent days on a catamaran sailing out over crystal blue water into the blazing horizon. We forgot all about looming work deadlines and failed to read the books we'd brought along. Instead, we communed with the vagabonds and fortune tellers at Mallory Square. Took the Conch Train. Visited Tennessee Williams and Hemingway. But mostly we just soaked up the atmosphere.

It's impossible to be in Key West for even a day and not realize it's like nowhere else. It's not just that it's laid-back, though it's that in spades. There's no advantage to putting on airs in Key West. Or to dropping names. It's truly the last egalitarian society—it really doesn't matter who you are. Not to mention it celebrates eccentricity with enthusiasm. You could sashay down Duval in your slippers and nighty, if it struck your fancy, and receive compliments. It's nothing short of liberating.

That Christmas turned out to be one of the most memorable that any of us had ever spent. And there was a subsequent irony. Little did I know that a few years later I would marry a fly-fishing captain with a passion for hunting down trophy fish in Keys waters. As a result, for several months each year, Key West would become my home. But I could never have predicted that I would fall in love with its storied past, learning of its wreckers, shrimpers, writers, and revolutionaries. It has become a part of my DNA.

These days it's hard for me to go to a restaurant like La Te Da and not imagine the dashing poet-revolutionary José Martí on the balcony, rousing his fellow Cubans against Spanish domination. Or to walk into Sloppy Joe's and not see journalist Martha Gellhorn perched on a bar stool, waiting to get her mitts on Hemingway. Key West is not just a retreat and a winter home.

It's a kind of living storybook in which each day brings past and present pleasures and surprises. It's a joy to share the island with you in *Key West: Paradise Found*, with the photos of Missy Janes to give the stories shape and color.

Ellen T. White

GETTY IMAGES

I

The Making of Paradise

When the late, great Jimmy Buffett first stepped onto Key West in 1971, according to legend, he was a long-haired musician, three years beyond a first album that no one remembered. His weekend in the island paradise was essentially an accident. Booked into a gig in Coconut Grove, Buffett had mixed up his dates and arrived two weeks early. To kill time, he and a fellow musician bar-hopped their way down Overseas Highway and landed in Key West. On arrival the duo headed to Mallory Square where crowds gathered each night to catch the elusive "green flash" as the sun dipped below the horizon line.

Buffett was taken with the sideshow at Mallory Square—barefoot musicians, tropical food vendors, and "old rummies" who blew on conch shells, ushering in the sunset. That night, in a time-honored tradition, Buffett and company "crawled" through the bars on Duval Street, where they were embraced by the tribe of local writers. Sleepless, Buffett ended up at the cemetery at dawn, communing with the ever-present ghosts of Key West. Buffett flew back to Miami a changed man. He claimed he had found home.

"It was completely virgin territory," he told a journalist, decades later. "Incredible characters, great bars. A different form of life, almost. It was still a wide-open town, where artists, straights, gays, shrimpers, sailors, criminals, and politicians all frequented the same bars." Buffett saved his paycheck and returned to Key West and played at local bars—notably the Chart Room—for free drinks. Ultimately, of course, he would write the hit song "Margaritaville," which summed up the Key West experience.

Many since have heeded Buffett's siren call, aiming to be "a free man (or woman) in paradise" for a weekend, a month, a season—even a lifetime. And while thrill-seekers no longer find Buffett, they still revel in the come-as-you-are town that Key

Among Friends: The late sculptor Seward Johnson appeared to take Key West's motto—"One Human Family"—to heart when he created *New Friends* in 2007. The sculpture of seven life-size figures has greeted visitors at various hotspots throughout Key West, the Southernmost Point and the Key West International Airport among them. Wherever it stands, the sculpture's remarkable presence has always said, "Whoever you are, you are welcome here." MISSY JANES

West has always been, where "live and let live" could be its motto, though "One Human Family" is the official line. Since its earliest days, Key West has shown its knack for reinvention, surviving hurricanes, fires, world wars, real estate development, and economic catastrophe on an epic scale. Through it all, Key West has never lost the mystery and romance that come with the territory.

Splendid Isolation

If Key West were not a good distance from civilization, the fabled Southernmost Point of the continental United States, it might have become just another humdrum tourist destination. It's surprising when you look at a map. It's the last island in a chain that swings out like a cat's tail to the west below Florida, reaching deep into the Gulf of Mexico. It's only 90 miles from Cuba, with which it shares kinship and history, and 130 miles from Miami, which wasn't even settled when Key West thrived.

Some say indigenous tribes—the Calusa and the Tequesta, namely—used Key West as a burial ground long before the Spanish land grab of the 1500s. This may be why the Spanish called it Bone Island, or Cayo Hueso, later anglicized to Key West. The fabled bones might also have been the remains of sailors whose ships had foundered on the treacherous reefs of the Florida Straits—a frequent occurrence back in the days before reliable charts and markers. Or not. Could be there were no bones at all.

It's a point of fact, though, that sailors dealt with headwinds, seasonal hurricanes, shallow waters, shoals, and tricky currents through the Florida Straits. And sometimes died there, their schooners sinking in fast water. Yet the Straits, with its powerful Gulf Stream, was the swiftest route for ships carrying cargo from the Gulf up the U.S. coastline.

Bahamians salvaged cargo from shipwrecks. "Privateers" also did for sponsor countries, such as Spain, and made a handsome living at it. Then there were pirates, who seized cargo, terrorizing their victims as a warning to others. The Caribbean was riddled with pirates when the U.S. bought Florida from the Spanish in 1819 for $2 million (the price of a decent house in Key West today). The U.S. Navy's Mosquito Fleet successfully rousted them out.

What John W. Simonton, an entrepreneur from Alabama, saw on a stopover in Key West in 1822 was that wrecking could be big business on a global scale. Key West, perched on the Straits due north, stood to benefit

GETTY IMAGES CRISTIANI

from ships that foundered—as many as one a week, if the wreckers were lucky. That same year, Simonton bought Key West from a Spanish grandee for a mere $2,000. The grandee sold it twice more in what was perhaps Florida's first recorded real estate scam.

A few months after Simonton laid his claim, Lieutenant Matthew Perry showed up and raised the American flag to claim Key West and established the first Navy presence. He called it Thompson Island after the U.S. Navy Secretary. The name didn't take. Key West it was, going forward.

A Wrecker's Playground

We're getting to the "wreckers," gentlemen of the salvaging business, though many would dispute the characterization. They were licensed by 1828 and honor-bound to rescue shipwrecked crew and cut a fair deal for the profits on the cargo, or face a judge in Key West's Federal Wreckers Court. The first wrecker to sidle up to a sinking ship struck a deal with the captain to split the profits—that is, provided the loot could be saved before it sank to the bottom.

A Wrecker's Town: *The Wreckers*, a sculpture by Miami artist James Mastin, is the crowning centerpiece of the Memorial Sculpture Garden near Mallory Square, which recognizes Key West's pioneering men and women. Wreckers salvaged cargo from sinking ships that had foundered on the reefs of the Florida Straits between Key West and Cuba, an important shipping lane. But unlike pirates, their close cousins, wreckers saved the lives of passengers, even when there was no financial incentive. The sculpture shows a young girl clinging to a wrecker's back, while another salvager hauls cargo. The first salvager to reach a sinking ship was designated the Master Wrecker who reaped the lion's share of the profits on a salvaging operation. MISSY JANES

"I expected to see a parcel of low, dirty, pirate-looking craft, officered and manned by a set of black-whiskered fellows, who carried murder in their very looks," wrote a traveling doctor of stepping aboard a wrecking vessel. But he found "fine, large schooners" in "first rate order" whose captains were "good humored sons of Neptune." Key West visitors will see the names of some of the notable wreckers around town—Geiger, Curry, Roberts, among them. They say the lookout tower at the Shipwreck Museum on a clear day will take you back there in time.

Not that there weren't bad apples among the bunch. The infamous John Jacob Housman—a New Yorker—was their poster boy. Famously, he stole his daddy's schooner and headed to Key West in hopes of gaming the wrecking system. He routinely swindled the unsuspecting but finally met his just deserts while working a wreck. Housman fell and was crushed between two vessels.

As Simonton had noted, Key West had a fine, deep-water port, protected from winds, where ships could lay up indefinitely. That magnificent harbor accommodates the deep-water draw of cruise ships today. But Simonton and his partners (John Whitehead, John Fleming, and Pardon Greene) smartly banked on its becoming a port of entry for U.S. Customs. They wasted no time in building the warehouses to accommodate the haul. An Egyptian mummy, the fossilized bones of a prehistoric sea monster, a railroad locomotive, and a herd of cavalry horses were among the more exotic cargo later recorded; more typically, it was cotton, Cuban coffee and sugar, wood, silver, and tobacco.

The call of "Wreck Ashore!" threw the town into action. Within a decade, as much as a staggering 90 percent of all imports and exports through territorial Florida were processed through Key West, with wrecking accounting for a good portion of this. The island's residents—wreckers, shipbuilders, lawyers, insurers, and chandlers, among them—would become among the wealthiest per capita in the country. Their grand houses were furnished in style with the spoils. The island's Oldest House on Duval is one of the few that survive.

Like the Gold Rush, Key West drew adventurers from the corners of the world. A visitor in 1831 described the town as it grew from a Navy installation into a commercial juggernaut, teeming with "persons from almost every country and speaking almost every variety of language." They brought with them "habits, manners, views and feelings, formed in different schools and in many instances totally contradictory."

Not surprisingly, Key West had a reputation for open-mindedness, the live-and-let-live attitude that survives today. European immigrants also benefited from the relatively progressive climate of the island, where nearly half the white citizens were foreign born. True, there were slaves, pre-Civil War; Fort Zachary Taylor was built on the backs of free labor. But nearly 20 percent of Florida's free blacks also lived there, although Key West had just two percent of the state's population.

Seizing the Day: A Union Town

Still, Key West was a southern town, with sympathies that aligned with the state of Florida—decidedly pro-slavery. For most Floridians, Abraham Lincoln's 1860 election was a catastrophe, "the beginning of the end," in the words of one newspaper. The governor called a convention to sort things out. On the morning of January 10, 1861, the gathered delegates voted 62 to 7 to secede from the Union. The news reached Key West two days later, internet connections not being what they are today.

Queasy with anxiety, Captain John Brannan, the ranking U.S. Army officer at Key West, repeatedly petitioned Washington for orders. On January 13, he could wait no longer. Shortly past midnight, he secreted his troops out of their barracks on the northeastern side of Key West. "In the dead of night," according to one soldier, he led his ragtag group of 42 men "by a route avoiding the town" to Fort Zachary Taylor, which still

The U.S. Navy presence has ebbed and flowed in Key West since 1823 and played a role in virtually all its conflicts, beginning with piracy, which Commodore David Porter eliminated with his Mosquito Fleet. During the Civil War, the Navy base kept Key West in Union hands, interdicting blockade runners to Confederate shores. The Navy suppressed slave shipping, illegal after 1808, and enforced customs law. In 1898 the U.S.S. *Maine* was sent from Key West to Havana, in response to tensions between Cuba and Spain, which gave rise to the Spanish-American War. During World War II, the Key West Navy base was used as a station for destroyers, submarines, surface patrol craft, and patrol seaplanes. Critical to the U.S. during the Cuban Missile Crisis in 1961, the Navy base was the closest U.S. military installation to Cuba. MISSY JANES

stands on the western shore. They met up with a small platoon of engineers and laborers that had agreed to help. Together they took the fort, still unfinished, and prepared to wait it out, barricaded in with provisions and water.

When Key Westers awoke, surprise!, they did so in a Union town—in fact, the only one south of the Mason-Dixon line. This didn't sit well with the majority. Many Key Westers left to serve the rebels—former Florida Senator Stephen Mallory, whose name you'll recognize, became the Confederacy's navy secretary.

From the Union point of view, capturing Key West was a strategic coup. All that made Key West a wrecker's town now served the Union at war. The Union army blockaded ships carrying supplies through the Straits and confiscated their cargo. The so-called Anaconda Plan starved out the South, effectively helping to win the war.

A Talent for Reinvention

Wrecking was in its prime at the outbreak of the Civil War, but the Industrial Revolution took it down. Steam power replaced sails. Navigational charts improved. Newly built railroads began to ship cargo. To the chagrin of wreckers, old lighthouses were repaired—and new ones were constructed, thanks to Congress. "Those damn lights," said a retired wrecker, "I wish they was all sunk beneath the sea!"

Wrecking continued, but not with the swagger it had in its glory years, though wrecking court, then in the Custom House, didn't actually disband until 1921. But existing industries more than flourished. Key Westers, accustomed to rebuilding after catastrophic hurricanes and fire, reinvented their town.

The island's natural salt ponds yielded bounty—the demand was great before refrigeration. Sea sponges had been discovered in the Florida Keys in the 1820s. A nasty business, sponging, in which harvesters beat and

Sea sponges were discovered in the Florida Keys in the 1820s and the industry took off with Key West exporting 2,000 tons of sponges a year all over the world. FLORIDA KEYS HISTORY CENTER—MONROE COUNTY LIBRARY

dried rank-smelling carcasses before turning them into a pliable product. After being test marketed in New York City in 1849, the industry took off. Key West exported 2,000 tons of sponges a year all over the world.

You won't find turtle soup on any menu today—at least, not legally. However, in the 1860s and '70s, a fad for turtle soup swept the country. "What champagne is to other wines, turtle is to other meats," according to an industry maven. While the Key West Kraals still exist, the turtles largely don't. Green Turtle Soup, a particular delicacy in England among swells, drove the species to near extinction.

But it was the Cuban cigar that changed everything.

The Road to Revolution: Cigar-Making

Ninety miles away from Key West, Cubans rose up against Spanish rule in what came to be known as the Ten Years' War (1868-78). Cubans—among them, cigar workers—sought safe haven in Key West where the climate was a fit. It was a U.S. tariff on imported cigars that proved to be Key West's making. The tax applied only to the finished product, not to tobacco. In a clever hack, the tobacco was still grown in Cuba, but factories cropped up all over the island to manufacture cigars. Key West returned to what it did so well: being a boom town.

By 1876, 29 cigar factories were producing 62 million cigars annually—the Gato Building on Simonton is a surviving relic. An influx of Cuban cigar makers and their families bumped the population to in excess of 18,000 by 1890, when Key West was counted as the largest and wealthiest city in Florida.

Tobacco Road: Many Cubans, notably cigar workers, fled to Key West during the fight against the Spanish for independence in the late 19th century. Among them was Cuban-born Eduardo Hildalgo Gato, who built a cigar factory on Simonton Street in 1884, becoming one of the most successful entrepreneurs in the business. At the cigar industries' peak in Key West in 1890, he employed 500 workers for whom he built dozens of cottages—the first viable industrial community in the U.S., which came to be known as El Barrio de Gato, or Gatoville. After his cigar factory was consumed by flames in 1915, Gato rebuilt the structure, a municipal building today. ELLEN T. WHITE

Cuba Libre: The San Carlos Hall on Ann Street was followed by the San Carlos Institute on Fleming in 1884, which was destroyed in the Great Fire of 1886 (reportedly started by Spanish agents at the cafe next door). It was at this San Carlos Institute on Duval Street, built in 1890, that poet revolutionary Jose Marti united the exile community to launch the final phase of Cuban independence. In its day, it has served as a political club, a school, an opera house, and a cultural center. In 1915, Anna Pavlova and the Russian Ballet appeared there. Today, the Spanish revival-style building with its sweeping rooms and marble floors is a museum of Cuban history and a spectacular venue for myriad cultural events held there. Its name honors Carlos Manuel de Cespedes, a plantation owner and the father of Cuban independence, who famously cried, "Cuba Libre!" from his balcony. MISSY JANES

Cigar workers also brought the revolutionary spirit from their island. Lectors or readers were hired to entertain factories full of cigar rollers by reading novels aloud. They swapped out *The Count of Monte Cristo* for the daily newspapers with glowing reports of a new kid in town: the magnetic José Martí. Martí, a Cuban journalist and poet, won over his countrymen with his revolutionary message. For conspiring against Spain, Martí was a man in exile.

Oh, to have been a fly on the wall when Martí spoke in Key West, which he did numerous times in 1891—from the Mallory Steamship dock, the Gato Building, the San Carlos Institute, and famously from the balcony of cigar manufacturer Teodoro Perez's home on Duval, today the hotel-restaurant La Te Da. Martí filled the revolutionary coffers with contributions from his countrymen. Key West's sizable Jewish population, whose antipathy for Spain dated back to the Inquisition, also rallied.

The Cuban War of Independence finally erupted in 1895. With unrest so close to shore, U.S. politicians took to biting their nails. (In fact, the Great Fire of 1886, which wiped out most of Key West's business district, was thought to have been the work of Spanish arsonists.) The U.S.S.

Maine, a Navy battleship, was sent to Key West and then on to Havana. On February 15, 1898, an explosion ripped through the forward. In under an hour the ship and many of its seamen sank to the bottom of the harbor.

The so-called Spanish-American War lasted just four months. "Remember the *Maine*!" was the rallying cry. The U.S. gained Puerto Rico and Guam in the struggle. Cuba, at last, won independence.

Paving the Way to Paradise

A man named Henry Flagler, a partner of John D. Rockefeller in the oil business, had a vision: extend the railroad from Miami down to Key West. Who doesn't love a tropical climate in the wintertime? Build it, and well-heeled visitors will come, was his theory. His luxurious Casa Marina hotel would greet them at the end of the line.

Seven years in the making, the so-called Eighth Wonder of the World was constructed over 128 miles and 42 bridges at a cost of $127 million, an amount that's almost impossible to imagine in dollars today. Dreaming of commerce, he created Trumbo Point—named for his chief engineer—out of landfill, with docks to accommodate shipping lines.

The Overseas Railroad was finally completed in 1912 with Flagler arriving in Key West on the first cars to a cheering crowd. But the Overseas Railroad didn't quite live up to the hype. By the 1930s, according to one account, the train chugged across the waters "carrying nothing, nowhere, for nobody."

The hurricane of 1935, a dead hit to the middle Keys, would wipe out the Overseas Railroad permanently—killing 200 people the train was sent to rescue. By 1930, construction of the Overseas Highway was approved, plunging Key West into irretrievable debt. But the highway promised to deliver sun-seekers to its shores. The ghostly remains of the railroad, which still runs alongside the highway, are an eerie reminder that the best-laid plans in Key West are at the mercy of weather.

The visionary industrialist Henry Flagler—depicted here by sculptor Seward Johnson—completed his railroad extension to Key West in 1912 and arrived on the first train to a cheering crowd of 10,000 onlookers.
MISSY JANES

The Birth of Pan Am Airlines: Pan Am pilots Huey Wells and Eddie Musick delivered 772 pounds of mail to Havana from Key West on October 28, 1927—the airline had won the mail contract just months before. International postal service was just the start of founder Juan Trippe's plans for his fledgling airline. He aimed to "provide mass air transportation for the average man at rates he can afford to pay." Pan Am Airlines would be the principal and largest international carrier in the U.S. until its demise in 1991, pioneering innovations like the jumbo jet and computerized reservations. It all started here in Key West at the Pan Am offices. Today, the historic building is the First Flight Island Restaurant and Southernmost Brewery. The restaurant's Crash Bar features a Sikorsky seaplane diving through the ceiling. MISSY JANES

A Party Town

Key West was always a thirsty town. William Hackley, who practiced law there in the 1820s, complained that the island was full of "vagabond sailors . . . who were usually drunk from the time of their arrival to their departure." Fistfights and duels were not uncommon, particularly without the civilizing influence of women, who "were in terribly short supply" in the frontier town. A lack of entertainment led naturally "to long sittings over 'the wine cup' at the dinner table."

Nearly a century later the temperance movement would strike terror in the hearts of saloon owners of Key West. Carrie Nation—the prohibition radical who vandalized saloons with a hatchet—visited Key West in 1908. She must have had a sense of humor, for she mailed to a friend a

GETTY IMAGES—DTIMIRAOS

Clothing Optional: Since its inception in 1979, Fantasy Fest has morphed into a cross between Mardi Gras and Burning Man—that is, a destination event in which some 75,000 revelers from around the planet pile into Key West in late October for a bacchanalia that has become legendary. Each year offers a theme: Va Va Voom, A-Conch-Alypse, Habitat for Insanity, Circuses and Sideshows, among them. For 10 days straight, parties abound. Clothing and sobriety are optional within the "Fantasy Zone." Fantasy Fest is the place where "grownups" allow their inner id to roam free without fear of arrest. It all culminates in a parade down Duval with competitive floats. Key Westers always party with purpose. Fantasy Fest has benefitted charities such as AIDS Help of Monroe County and SPCA and crowns each year's two top fundraisers—the King and Queen of Fantasy Fest—in a two-hour coronation ceremony. Those who've had "tutu much to drink" chase hangovers with bottomless mimosas and Bloody Marys the morning after. ANDY NEWMAN—FLA-KEYS.COM

color postcard produced in Key West that read "All Nations are welcome except Carrie." But the die was cast. In January of 1919 the 18th Amendment banned the manufacture, transportation, and sale of liquors. Not that Key West gave a damn.

Key Westers bragged that their town was the only one in Florida without a Prohibition agent—true, that. A traveling agent periodically breezed through town and made arrests. Visitors who planned a trip to Havana for a good time soon learned that Key West was as far as they needed to go. Speakeasies such as Pena's and Ramonin's cropped up—one of the most popular was tucked away in the Southernmost House.

Rum running from Cuba became a popular pastime sport—not to mention a means of earning a living in a Depression economy. Everyone got into the game, including the Coast Guard. Hemingway's only Key West novel, *To Have and Have Not*, chronicled a fishing guide eking out a living as a rumrunner in hard times. Writer John Dos Passos, a frequent visitor, called Key West a place of "agreeable calm and gently colored with Bacardi."

To this day, Key West remains a place to cut loose; some start with the bar cart on the plane down. Bar hoppers brag that they started at the Green Parrot, moved to Sloppy Joe's, and ended up naked in the Garden of Eden hours later. The "Duval Crawl" is a rite of passage for vacationers visiting Key West for the first time; many never abandon the practice. But the truth is that any excuse for a party is good enough in Key West.

The Hemingway Effect

With the stock market crash of 1929, the United States hit the skids. But Key West had been on a downward descent for a long time. Cigar factories relocated to Tampa. In the final straw, the army and navy pulled up their stakes after the Great War, taking the paychecks that had been vital to keeping the town afloat. And this suited some visitors just fine.

Describing Key West as "desperately unprosperous," writer John Dos Passos found it to be "a swell little jumping off place," unspoiled by tourists and Prohibition agents. It was a "blessing," he concluded, that there was "nothing to do on the island." He persuaded Ernest Hemingway of the island's charms, saying it was "like no place in Florida"—as true today as it was then.

Ernest Hemingway in Key West FLORIDA KEYS HISTORY CENTER—MONROE COUNTY LIBRARY

On the brink of fame, Hemingway returned from Paris with a new wife when he ferried into Key West in 1928 to pick up a new car. By the time the car was ready weeks later, Hemingway had fallen for the fishing and the locals, who traded in his special brand of authenticity.

"Nobody believes me when I say I'm a writer," he wrote his editor, Maxwell Perkins. "They think I represent Big Northern Bootleggers or Dope Peddlers." He invited his "mob" to stay and bolstered the economy with his bar tabs, fishing, and construction projects. The fixer-upper he bought on Whitehead Street, originally built by the wrecker Asa Tift, is now, of course, a public shrine. He wrote many of his celebrated books in Key West. The title character of *The Old Man and the Sea*, for which he won the Pulitzer Prize, is a composite of the island's characters.

Robert Frost, Wallace Stevens, Archibald MacLeish, Clifford Odets, and even the legendary Sara and Gerald Murphy passed through, drawn by reports of Key West's charming but seedy obscurity. The literary community declared Key West "ruined" by Franklin Roosevelt's New Dealers, who came to the "rescue."

Painting the Town: The Depression Era

How broke was Key West? Key West was so broke that they turned off the streetlights and stopped collecting the garbage. Citizens lined up for food rations. The Overseas Highway brought tourists lured by a bargain vacation, but its construction had squeezed the town out of its last dime. Government handouts were keeping the island going—until the arrival in 1934 of Julius Stone, a Harvard-educated New Dealer who envisioned Key West as a rival Bermuda, then the popular getaway.

According to a historian, Stone saw "sunshine, a frost-free climate, interesting architecture, a culturally and racially mixed population, a romantic past filled with pirates and wreckers" begging for tourist dollars. Bankrupt Key West was thrown into a "state of emergency," after

The Key West Art Center Gallery is the successor to the Community Art Center established during the Depression by the WPA artists who were sent to the island to spruce up the town. MISSY JANES

which Stone took control. Scores of volunteers tossed piles of dead foliage, razed shacks, and litter. Teams of children raked seaweed and debris from the beaches in a coordinated effort that one observer said resembled a "utopian society."

Stone invited artists, supported by Roosevelt's Works Progress Administration, to transform the town with murals and paintings. They stayed and formed the Key West Community Art Center—later, the Key West Art Center—ultimately turning the island into the thriving art colony it is today. Postcards, brochures, and advertisements promoted Key West as an exotic destination, a Caribbean island with domestic currency. The well-heeled took to it. It was possible to find "a duke, an anarchist, and a fan dancer," according to radio personality Elmer Davis, "on adjacent bar stools." Residents were encouraged to spruce up their houses and rent them out.

Famously, Stone introduced bicycles and Bermuda shorts to Key West, leading by example. When he showed up in his shorts at Raul's nightclub, the owner barred him from the door for being "naked." Stone's fashion sense stuck. To this day, the goal in Key West is to wear as little as you can without getting arrested.

Trained on Tourism: It's hard to tell where the Conch Train is coming from or where it's going, but this much we know: it's a universal presence in Old Town Key West. Seven days a week since 1958, that brightly colored locomotive has twisted and turned down the narrow streets of the island, uncovering its many mysteries over a PA system. Is the Key West cemetery haunted? Did a mayor of Key West really waterski to Havana? Why is the legendary bar called Sloppy Joe's and did Hemingway really meet his third wife there? "It's a crash course in Key West history," claimed Jimmy Buffett. "You needn't feel embarrassed riding the Conch Train," says a popular guidebook. "A strange cloak of invisibility is dropped over yourself as you board." MISSY JANES

Booms and Busts

Shrimp were discovered off the Dry Tortugas in 1949, leading to the "Pink Gold Rush." Trawlers regularly hauled eight million pounds out of the water each year—so many trawlers rushed to Key West in the '50s and '60s, it was reported, that you could walk from one end of the seaport to the other without touching water. Plentiful shrimp kept fishermen, fish markets, and packers in the black for decades, but by the late 1980s the waters were overfished. Shrimp had gone the way of turtles.

Once again, the real drain on Key West was the closure in 1974 of the Naval Base, which at the time reached from the waterfront up to Boca Chica. The Navy had ebbed and flowed in and out of Key West since the wrecker era, but backlash from Vietnam forced changes. Forty percent of Key West's population disappeared with the Navy's departure, leaving the proprietors of bars, restaurants, shops, and services twiddling their thumbs. The island was forced to reinvent itself once more.

Hippies discovered Key West in droves, turning the island into "Haight-Ashbury South." The playwright Tennessee Williams, now a beloved resident of Key West, remarked that Duval Street after dark had become "the final retreat of the 'flower children.'" At the "long-haired convention" in Mallory Square, unpermitted musicians were arrested for playing. Restaurants and bars obligingly made space. An unknown named Jimmy Buffett headlined at Ophelia's. According to the newspapers, he "made everyone feel like one big happy family."

Shrimp Boats in Key West FLORIDA KEYS HISTORY CENTER—MONROE COUNTY LIBRARY

Sex, Drugs, & . . .

Drugs were an open secret in Key West. As with Prohibition, drug use was largely ignored until a gangland-style murder in Key Largo shook up the authorities. In the most sensational case of the decade, state narcotics agents and U.S. Customs officers launched "Operation Conch," which landed four policemen, a detective, a city attorney, and, notably, the fire chief—a local character named Bum Farto, whose custom plates on his convertible read "El Jefe."

In Key West's own Jimmy Hoffa saga, Bum Farto disappeared days before he was due to be sentenced. Was it a Mafia murder? An escape? Nothing was found when they dredged Key West harbor. "Where Is Bum Farto?" became a ubiquitous tee shirt, worn on stage by Jimmy Buffett.

In the era of free love, music, and drugs, Key West was ripe for rediscovery by a new generation of writers. Among them was Thomas McGuane, author of the Key West novel *Ninety-two in the*

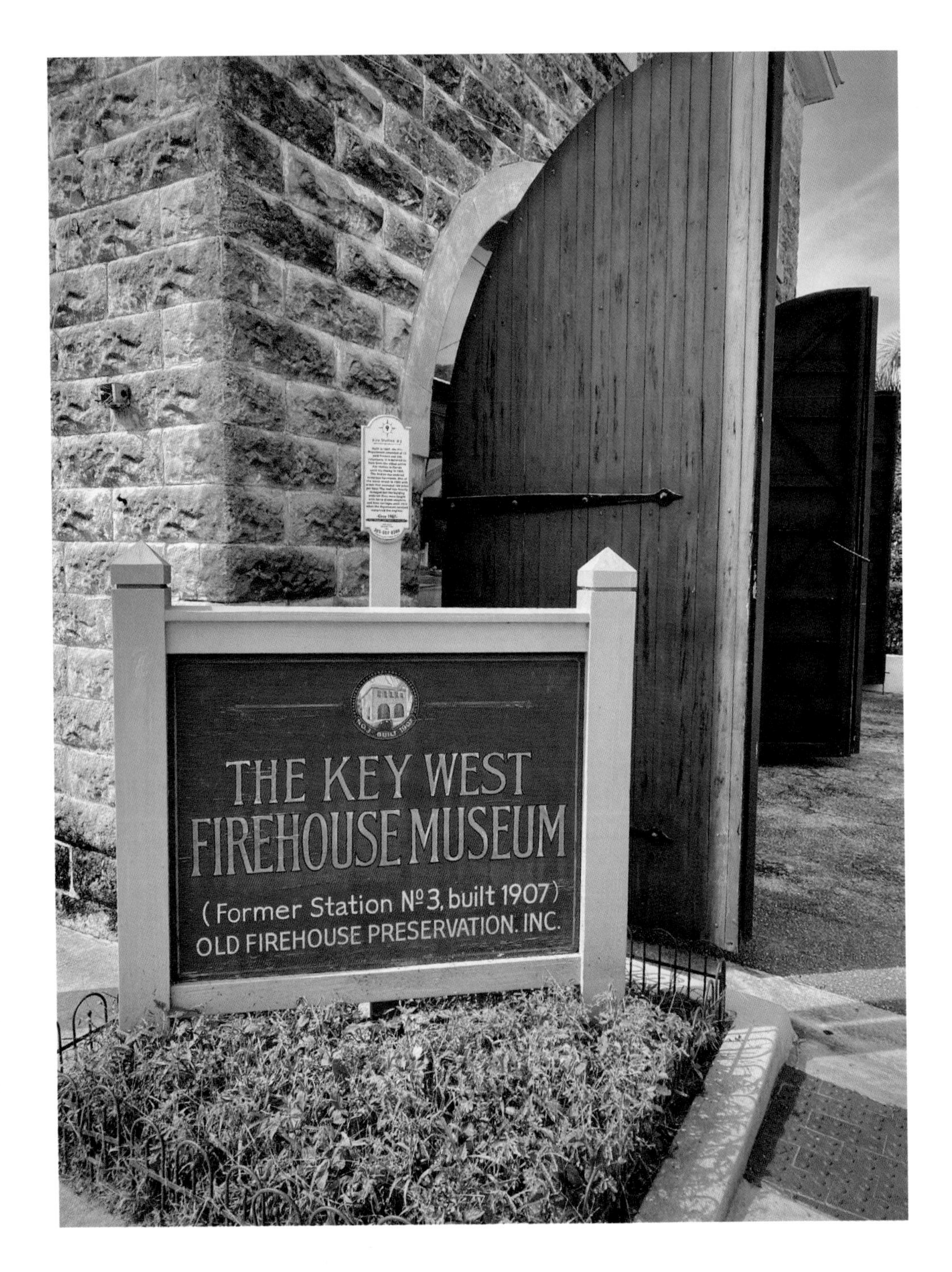

Hot History: The "hottest historic attraction in town," the Firehouse Museum is a trove of information on Key West's intimate relationship with fire—most famously, the Great Fire of 1886. The day the fire raged through Key West, stoked by high winds, the department's only engine was in New York for repairs. Most of the business district of Key West was destroyed, killing seven people. But the fires of 1843, 1859, and 1863, among others, also had dire consequences. The Firehouse Museum, formerly Firehouse #3, touts vintage fire gear, an original bunk house, antique badges, and a 1906 cemetery fire bell, as well as the desk of former Fire Chief Bum Farto. "If these walls could talk," they like to say at the museum, "you wouldn't believe the stories." Farto disappeared in 1976 after his conviction for selling drugs to an undercover agent in a sting operation. MISSY JANES

From left to right, writers Tom McGuane, Truman Capote, Tennessee Williams, and James Kirkwood hobnobbing at Louie's Backyard in Key West. FLORIDA KEYS HISTORY CENTER—MONROE COUNTY LIBRARY

Shade. "You were in a sympathetic culture to be an artist," said McGuane, viewed by his friends as Hemingway's second coming. "It was a real chance to find out a lot in a short time in a small space." And to have fun while doing it.

McGuane hobnobbed with Buffett, Jim Harrison, Phil Caputo, and Hunter S. Thompson—dubbed Club Mandable, for reasons nobody can now remember. He famously romanced the two female leads on the set of *92 in the Shade*, shot in Key West, while his wife took up with the film's protagonist. Sex, drugs, and rock & roll had reached Key West, but the idea of open marriage was in its infancy. "They were the naughty years," writer Carl Hiaasen remembered fondly. "You're at the end of America," said Harrison. "It's the tropics and it doesn't, largely, have much to do with the rest of Florida."

By the 1980s, Tennessee Williams was Key West's revered literary lion—though, increasingly, he was a less than sober presence. "I want you to know that the town is literally swarming with men in uniform," Williams had written to a friend on his arrival in 1941, "mostly sailors in very tight white pants . . . it is extremely interesting." He had introduced the town to a gay population, who by the 1970s were key to the town's restoration in large part as proprietors of Key West's inns, shops, and restaurants.

Viva the Conch Republic

In a complete reversal, Cuban President Fidel Castro announced in 1980 that anyone who wanted to leave Cuba could do so, immediately. The announcement spurred a mass exodus. Cuban Americans in Key West and Miami organized transportation; the *USGC Ingham*, currently docked at Truman Waterfront, was pressed into service. In the first two weeks of the "Mariel Boatlift," 14,000 refugees landed in Key West. News reports showed them sleeping in doorways and begging for food. U.S. President Jimmy Carter called it a disaster area.

In the spring of 1982, U.S. Border Patrol blocked the top of the Overseas Highway leading into the Keys, searching for drugs and Cuban refugees. The whole enterprise stopped traffic dead in its tracks for 19 miles.

The flag of the newly anointed Conch Republic was unveiled in 1982. Why conch? A conch is, of course, a sea snail. But "Conchs" also referred to Americans loyal to the British who fled to the Bahamas around the time of the Revolution (but would rather "eat conch than pay British taxes"). The term traveled with Bahamians who moved to Key West later on. Since then, it has described a Key West native—anyone who is born and bred on the island. The flag has come to signify the independent spirit of Key West, forever and always the proud Conch Republic. FLORIDA KEYS HISTORY CENTER—MONROE COUNTY LIBRARY

A modern, rainbow edition of the flag of the Conch Republic, first unveiled in 1982. MISSY JANES

Motorists sat on the highway in 82-degree heat for up to four hours. Vacationers promptly canceled their vacation plans.

"They're treating us like a foreign country," said Dennis Wardlow, the city's mayor, "so we might as well become one." The bold plan was to secede from the Union, declare war on the U.S., fire a shot, and then surrender, after which the Conch Republic would demand $1 billion in foreign aid.

At noon on April 23, 1982, Key Westers gathered to watch Wardlow officially raise the new flag of the new "nation." The brown pelican was designated as the republic's bird, the hibiscus its flower. The official drink, obviously with lime, was debated among bartenders up until press time. A phalanx of reporters stood by as Wardlow ceremoniously broke a loaf of Cuban bread over the head of a man dressed as a sailor and promptly surrendered to the Navy Commander. The republic lasted one day but the press coverage was priceless for tourism. Key West calls itself the Conch Republic to this day, still waves its flag, and proudly touts its independence.

Ruling the Roost: Woe be to the man (or woman) who does not yield to the ubiquitous chickens and roosters of Key West, which collectively give new meaning to the term free range. This protected status, though unofficial, probably accounts for the gypsy fowls' brazen air of entitlement—even dogs run in the other direction rather than tangle with them. They are descendants of the Cubalaya cock-fighting breed, brought from Cuba to the island for food and sport in the late 19th century. "The feral fowl seem like the perfect metaphor for Key West," claims a visitor, "historic, colorful, sort of wild, a little noisy and occasionally annoying." MISSY JANES

II

Historic Destinations

A visitor's town to its core, Key West has long since kitted itself out with all the pleasures typically associated with this: picturesque guest houses, spas, aspirational dining, an abundance of shops with mementos of the time spent there. But it is the history that makes Key West what it is today. In league with Nantucket Island, Boston, and even Rome, Key West doesn't count its past as done. History lives nestled alongside the present—in its abundance of landmarks, museums, architecture, forts, cemeteries, and oft-told tales.

"It's hard to walk around Key West and not to feel its history rumbling beneath your feet," wrote William McKeen in *Mile Marker Zero*, his literary history of Key West. Just look up and note its streets; not a single one in Old Town was named at random, beginning with Simonton, after the island's visionary founder. To truly understand Key West, follow the trail. From the wreckers to writers, boom town to bust, Key West has always been a wild ride. Its historic destinations mark the channel, giving the past its weight and color.

Southernmost Point

If you need hardcore evidence that you've touched down in Key West, a selfie at the Southernmost Point buoy should do the trick. The striking yellow, red, and black buoy trumpets Key West's proud claim to being the southernmost point of the continental United States—just 90 miles from Cuba, as the crow flies. The 20-ton buoy replaced the multiple wooden signs that were repeatedly stolen as souvenirs. When the new buoy was dedicated in 1983, Key West's Director of Monuments invited Ronald Reagan, promising to rename adjacent South Street after the president. That South Street remains as it was then is perhaps testament to how seriously the White House took the invitation. GETTY IMAGES—S. GREG PANOSIAN

Mallory Square

The best show in town can be found every evening on Mallory Square, where crowds gather to watch the sun dip below the horizon line. Sunset's fabled "green flash" might be elusive, but the fire eaters, fortune tellers, stilt men, body painters, balloon animal vendors, jugglers, and break dancers are not. The tradition began in the 1960s, when "hippies" gathered and were occasionally jailed for playing music without a permit.

Many visitors since have begun their wild Key West adventure here—famously, singer Jimmy Buffett, according to legend. The nightly circus has become such an important part of Key West that often cruise ships, with special exceptions, pull away from the pier two hours before the sun slips away, returning only after dark, if at all. MISSY JANES

The Southernmost House

The Southernmost House—aka, The Mansion On The Sea—stands at the Atlantic's edge, a pale pink Queen Anne-style confection against blue skies. Judge Jeptha Vining Harris built the mansion for $250,000, a small fortune in 1897 dollars. His wife was the youngest daughter of the millionaire wrecker William Curry, who likely contributed funds.

Secret passageways leading from each room were built to avoid Seminole attack, or so it's rumored. If they existed, they must have come in handy when the Southernmost House became a speakeasy during Prohibition. Al Capone ran rum from Cuba out of the mansion, and gangsters and celebrities on their way to Cuba congregated here.

By 1939, the mansion was a Cuban-style nightclub called Cafe Cayo Hueso. Ernest Hemingway frequented the club. Tennessee Williams, Gore Vidal, Charles Lindbergh, Louis Armstrong, Truman Capote, Gloria Swanson, and Tallulah Bankhead were also among the carousing celebrities. But by 1954, owner Hilario Ramos, a liquor distributor, reclaimed the house as his residence.

Politically connected in his native Spain and the U.S., Hilario hosted five U.S. presidents at the Southernmost House—namely, Truman, Eisenhower, Kennedy, Nixon, and Carter. King Juan Carlos of Spain came calling, touching down on the helicopter pad especially built for the purpose. Composer Leonard Bernstein was looking for a place to get away during the '50s and lived briefly on the second floor, where he allegedly wrote *West Side Story*.

A leader in the preservation movement, Hilario's son Charles Ramos turned the Southernmost House into a swanky hotel. Today, guests steep themselves in Southernmost history by booking rooms in the house or the guest cottages nearby. ANNETTE HOLMSTROM

The Oldest House Museum

For aficionados of the wrecking era of Key West, the Oldest House on Duval Street is a remarkable relic of the bygone era. No other intact home predates this structure. As such, it is one of a very few houses to have survived the Great Fire of 1886, which consumed 80 percent of Key West, not to mention the steady barrage of hurricanes, floods, and all manner of punishing elements routinely visited on the island.

The house was built in 1825 on Whitehead Street by Richard Cussans, a merchant and a ship's carpenter, born in the Bahamas. Cussans's airtight ship's carpentry work contributed to the structure's survival. Sometime in the mid-1830s, the house was moved to Duval, which had been little more than a salt pond until the ground shifted in 1829.

By the 1840s it was the home of wrecker Captain Francis Watlington, his wife, Emilene, and their bevy of daughters. The Francis Watlington House, as it has since been called, is chock full of period furniture, ship models, and documents, such as original wrecker log books. Only a quick look is needed to understand the domestic discomforts of the time, even among the wealthiest families. As was the custom, a separate cookhouse, still intact, was built in the rear to protect the main house from fire.

Descendants of the Watlington family lived in the house until 1972, when it was bought and eventually turned over to the Old Island Restoration Foundation. A museum today, the house and its spectacular gardens are a marvel of peace and civility in the center of Old Town.

The Oldest House in Key West, as seen from the garden. MISSY JANES

A cookhouse was usually a separate structure in the grander houses of the 19th century as insurance against fire taking everything.

MISSY JANES

The Oldest House, charmingly rendered for postcards sold on the island. FLORIDA KEYS HISTORY CENTER—MONROE COUNTY LIBRARY

Harry S. Truman's Little White House

Truman House MISSY JANES

One of Truman's presidential limousines, a 1950 Ford Lincoln Cosmopolitan with "suicide doors." MISSY JANES

When Harry S. Truman first visited Key West in the fall of 1946, he had been U.S. President for 19 months, stepping up after FDR's death in 1945. He was thoroughly drained—near collapse from stress and the effects of a lingering cold, for which a warm climate was prescribed. He arrived at the Boca Chica naval air station on the presidential airplane, popularly known as Sacred Cow. Over the course of his presidency, he spent 11 working vacations in Key West at the "Little White House" for a total of 175 days and even returned after his term ended.

Originally built in 1880, the house was a duplex on the base used to house Navy brass. But in 1911, it was converted to the home you now see with attractive louvered wrap-around porches. The house is now outfitted with furnishings related to the Truman era—a rare study in 1950s decor. It's not hard to imagine the plainspoken Truman, his wife, Bess, and their daughter, Margaret, relaxing among the chintz and floral wallpapers.

Rumor has it that Truman famously nipped down to the kitchen each morning for a shot of bourbon in his orange juice—a practice that astonished his housekeepers. He ventured forth from the Little White House for a brisk walk down Whitehead Street to Wall and back, paying for his Cuban coffee with an autographed dollar. In his down time, Truman played poker with staffers at the vast, felt-covered table you'll still find in the bar. But dare to sit in one of the chairs and you'll be shown the door.

From his perch in Key West, Truman was in constant touch with world leaders. He developed the Marshall Plan, key to European recovery after World War II, and dealt with a coal miners' strike, the Cold War with the Soviet Union, and the Korean War. His desk bears his motto, "The Buck Stops Here"; there was no rest for weary presidents, even in Key West.

The Margaret Truman Launderette, on the corner of Truman and Margaret, was not named after the presidential daughter, who nonetheless appreciated the joke. ELLEN T. WHITE

Curry Mansion

Few rags-to-riches stories equal that of true "Conch" William Curry. Born in Green Turtle Cay in the Bahamas in 1821, Curry arrived in Key West as a penniless lad of 16, brandishing a keen sense of destiny. He worked briefly as a clerk and served in the Seminole War before joining the lucrative business of salvaging. Curry was no ordinary wrecker. Over the years, he enlarged his scope to ice manufacturing, bonded warehouses, general merchandising,

MISSY JANES

shipbuilding, and chandlery, becoming Florida's first millionaire. "His capacity for making safe and lucrative investments," wrote a historian, "amounted to genius."

Perhaps we can forgive Curry for commissioning an ostentatious solid gold table service for 24 from Tiffany & Co. (a lifelong dream!)—particularly on learning that he provided his children with homes of their own, resulting in some of the most interesting architecture on the island. The Dr. J. Yates Porter House, the Southernmost House, the Woman's Club, Fogarty Mansion, Robert Oliver Curry Mansion, and the George Curry Mansion are all due to William's largesse. With Curry's own house at 511 Caroline Street, they are collectively the "Curry Mansions."

Curry built his own mansion in 1869, on the site the family had homesteaded since 1855. According to urban legend, the key lime pie was born in the kitchen there, the invention of a cook known only as Aunt Sally (likely the wife of William's oldest son, Charles). In 1903, William's son Milton gutted the house and rebuilt it as a white Georgian revival mansion in the image of a Newport "cottage." The architectural embellishments are a grab bag of American styles—a New England widow's walk, the ornate trellises and balustrades of New Orleans, and the colonnades of the South. Operating as a bed-and-breakfast today, the Curry Mansion Inn is furnished in Victorian style.

GETTY IMAGES—IRINA MIRWAN

Audubon House & Tropical Garden

In the 1820s and '30s, the artist and naturalist John James Audubon set off on his epic quest across the country, ambitiously recording bird species. In Florida alone, Audubon identified 52 birds that were unfamiliar to him, choosing 18 to render in his life-sized drawings—among them, the Key West quail dove, the mangrove cuckoo, the roseate spoonbill, the blue-headed pigeon, and the brown pelican. Audubon's portfolio of 435 hand-colored prints was published as the celebrated *The Birds of America*.

Did Audubon ever visit the house named for him? In a word, no. The house at 205 Whitehead Street, completed in 1849, was built by John Huling Geiger, a master wrecker. Audubon, however, visited in 1832 and stayed aboard the *Marion*, the ship on which he sailed down the coast of Florida. But Audubon's drawing of a white-crowned pigeon shows a rough-leaved cordia (or geiger tree) found at this address, connecting the artist to his public shrine.

Before Audubon took over, four generations of Geigers lived here. The last lived without electricity or running water and pulled up groceries in a basket to the second floor. His spirit continues to hover over the third floor, along with other oddities documented by paranormal experts. Geiger's youngest son, Charles, occasionally taps the shoulder of those who pass by. Children's voices and laughter have been recorded, and photos show people enjoying a ghostly meal outside on the porch.

The house was slated for demolition in 1958 to make way for a gas station. But it was saved by Mitchell Wolfson, a Key West native and Miami collector. Its restoration, completed in 1960, was so successful it started the restoration movement of Old Town Key West. A highlight of the Audubon House is its one-acre tropical gardens where orchids, bromeliads, rare tropical palms, and crotons grow in profusion.

MISSY JANES

Bahama Village

GETTY IMAGES—BRUCE YUANYUE BI

Bahama Village sprawls over a 12-block area southwest of Whitehead Street, marked with an arch over Petronia bearing its legend. Settled in the mid-19th century by mainly Black Bahamian fishermen, shipbuilders, and wreckers, the area is rarely called out on maps, even those of the shamelessly commercial variety. But it is a wonderfully authentic part of Key West, with modest, brightly painted houses, neat yards, tiny stores, and a proliferation of churches.

In spite of significant gentrification, in the form of shops, the neighborhood has kept its charm. A visitor who happens upon it might still feel a sense of discovery. Chickens and roosters roam as if they own the place, which in a sense they do. They are the descendants of the cockfighters that arrived with the cigar industry. Hemingway apparently frequented the bars, restaurants, impromptu boxing rings, and cockfighting events in this part of town. Today, one of its chief claims to fame is the restaurant Blue Heaven, which has turned waiting for a table for brunch into an extreme sport.

Custom House: The Key West Art & Historical Society

The wrecking years were more than good to Key West. By 1882 the city's annual revenue was greater than that of all other Florida ports combined—mind-blowing when you stop to think of it. As the city's customs operations outgrew their small wooden headquarters near the harbor, the vast four-story red brick Custom House now flanking Mallory Square was planned and completed in 1891. It was built in the "Richardson Romanesque" style, after architect Henry Hobson Richardson, whose public buildings were the era's gold standard in design.

The building originally housed customs, the post office, and the federal court. Famously, it was the site of the inquiry into the sinking of the U.S.S. *Maine* in Havana harbor, the incident that plunged the U.S. into the Spanish-American War in 1898. Yet for years during the 20th century the brick beauty was abandoned—even as it was folded into the National Register of Historic Places. Talk of turning it into a yacht club or an upscale resort came to naught, thankfully. Today, it is the forever home of the Key West Art & Historical Society, which undertook its renovation and re-opened its doors in 1999.

The Key West Art & Historical Society brings to life the vast and colorful history, art, people, and events of the Florida Keys, turning the building into the bustling hub of culture on Mallory Square. Its collections and exhibitions cover subjects as varied as the Works Progress Administration, Ernest Hemingway's life on the island, and the woodcarvings of Mario Sanchez, a popular Key West artist, as well as the industries in which the island prospered. KWAHS doesn't stop there. It also oversees the Key West Lighthouse, the Fort East Martello Museum, and the Tennessee Williams Museum, giving form and substance to 200 years of Key West history.

MISSY JANES

Key West Cemetery

Suitably haunted, the Key West Cemetery is especially popular at night, when the spirits are restless. Dare to sit on a grave or otherwise dishonor the dead, and the apparition of a Bahamian woman will make you sorry. In evidence is the Key Westers' famous sense of humor. "I told you I was sick," reads one gravestone; another bears the legend, "I'm Just Resting My Eyes." The dearly departed never leave Key West—they live among us as spirits and legends, almost as palpably as if they were still alive.

Like much else in Key West, the graveyard was moved from its original location, near the lighthouse, after the 1846 hurricane blasted through, exhuming bodies—a gruesome sight not to be dwelt on here. The current 19-acre cemetery at the foot of Solares Hill, the high point of Key West, was established in 1847. As in New Orleans, many of the graves are built above ground. At 100,000 graves, the cemetery has four times the population of Key West. Your application to secure a plot will be refused, even if your great granddaddy was a salvager.

Many folks of significance are buried here, among them wrecker William Curry and Joe Russell, Hemingway's fishing guide and Sloppy Joe's proprietor. An enclosure is devoted to the unknown soldiers who perished in the explosion of the U.S.S. *Maine* in Havana harbor. The place is as democratic as Key West—all manner of Bahamian mariners, Cuban cigar makers, soldiers, Jews, Protestants, millionaires, and paupers have come to rest within shouting distance of each other.

There's also the bizarre tale of Count Carl Von Cosel, who stole from the cemetery the body of Elena Milagro Hoyos, a girl on whom he was fixated. The Count kept her preserved body—decked out in a wedding dress—in his bed for seven years, until her outraged family caught wind of it. She was reinterred at a secret location that the perpetually mourning Von Cosel could not find.

MISSY JANES

African Cemetery at Higgs Beach

"Near this site lie the remains of 294 African men, women, and children who died in Key West in 1860," reads a wrought-iron marker on the edge of Higgs Beach—a story that has broken the hearts of many. In the summer of that year, the U.S. Navy rescued 1,432 Africans from three ships engaged in the illegal slave trade on their way to Cuba. The Navy brought the freed slaves ashore, and townspeople provided food, shelter, and medical care. But so unsanitary and inhumane were the conditions aboard the rescued ships that many died sometime later. They are memorialized by the monument that charts their passage across the Atlantic and the subsequent repatriation of the survivors to Liberia.

MISSY JANES

Casa Marina

"I have been down here actually for a week but it seems as if I had never been anywhere else and never particularly wanted to be anywhere else," wrote the poet Wallace Stevens in 1930 while perched above sapphire Atlantic waters at the Casa Marina. From the moment it opened on New Year's Eve in 1920, the Casa Marina was the height of glam, usurping the claim La Concha on Duval had to the title.

The Casa Marina was the dream of tycoon Henry Flagler, whose Florida Railroad Extension, touted as the Eighth Wonder of the World, chugged into Key West in 1912. Along the railroad's route, Flagler created "halls of joy," hotels that catered to the well-heeled. He would not live to see his Casa at the end of the line. Nonetheless, Thomas Hastings and John M. Carrère, architects of New York's Metropolitan Opera House, honored every detail of Flagler's distinctive vision in a Spanish Renaissance-style palace with wide-open loggias and impeccable gardens. President Warren G. Harding was one of the first guests. Rita Hayworth, Robert Frost, Rudy Vallee, and John Philip Sousa were among the early celebrities who sought refuge and luxury within its hurricane-proof walls.

Casa Marina has seen a succession of owners over the years, including the military. During the 1960s and '70s the old Casa was abandoned and left for broke; later restoration efforts revived it. Since 2009, it's been a Hilton hotel. Henry Flagler would be pleased to see that its impressive lobby—with beamed ceilings and hardwood floors—is exactly as he imagined it when he planned the palace so long ago.

ELLEN T. WHITE

The architecture of Casa Marina's lobby was built as tycoon Henry Flagler imagined it. MISSY JANES

Key West Butterfly & Nature Conservancy

ELLEN T. WHITE

Owners George Fernandez and Sam Trophia took a leap of faith when they realized their dream: to create the Key West Butterfly and Nature Conservatory. The duo bought a Victorian on southern Duval, and transformed its interior into a glass-enclosed environment. The place is replete with 60 species of butterflies, 20 exotic birds, cascading waterfalls, flowering plants, and a gazebo. Two celebrity flamingoes, Rhett and Scarlett, roam the garden. The Conservatory, which opened in 2003, is a respite from beaches, bars, and crowds smack in the middle of all the Old Town action. The owners aim to transport visitors, beginning with the motto, "Excite Your Senses, Expand Your Mind."

MISSY JANES

ODE TO THE ARTS AND LETTERS

Hemingway House

MISSY JANES

Disenchanted by the U.S., Ernest Hemingway lived in Paris during the 1920s among fellow ex-pat writers, dubbed the Lost Generation by Gertrude Stein. By 1928, however, he longed to return home, or at least stateside. He complained to fellow writer John Dos Passos of Paris's unceasing rain and cold. Go to Key West, Dos Passos advised. Where Hemingway goes, legend follows.

Casting off his first wife, Hadley, Hemingway decamped to the U.S. by steamer, his pregnant new wife, Pauline, on his arm. Eventually, they ferried into Key West to pick up a car—a new Ford Model A, a gift from Pauline's rich uncle, Gus Pfeiffer. The car wouldn't be ready for six weeks, the dealer advised, but the apartment above the dealership was theirs if they were willing to wait it out.

MISSY JANES

Like so many before and since, Hemingway was instantly enchanted by Key West. "Christ, this is a fine country!", he wrote to a friend. "Have been catching tarpon, barracuda, jack, red snappers," including "the biggest tarpon" landed in Key West that season. In 1931, the Hemingways bought a fixer-upper at 907 Whitehead Street, a Spanish Colonial mansion built in 1851 by the wrecker Asa Tift. Hemingway wrote in the mornings in his studio loft by the pool, the first on the island.

MISSY JANES

Key West was a town "on the skids" during the Depression—the "San Tropez of the poor," Hemingway called it. His "mob" of friends came to stay. Between remodeling projects, fishing, and drinking, the Mob kept Key West afloat. Hemingway's literary output was nothing short of remarkable. During his time in Key West, Hemingway wrote *A Farewell to Arms* and *To Have and Have Not*, as well as *Death in the Afternoon*, *The Green Hills of Africa*, and the short stories "The Short Happy Life of Francis Macomber" and "The Snows of Kilimanjaro."

Later, Key West friends and his adventures aboard his boat the *Pilar* formed the basis of *The Old Man and the Sea*, for which he won the Pulitzer Prize. During those years Hemingway became an international public figure. When the tour brochure labeled his house 18th on a list of 48 things to see in Key West, Hemingway put up the six-foot wall that surrounds the place today.

Of all the bars Hemingway frequented—and there were many—only Sloppy Joe's, then owned by friend and fishing guide Joe Russell, survives. (The watering trough for the famous six-toed cats at the Hemingway House was the urinal at the original Greene Street location of Sloppy's.) According to legend, when journalist Martha Gellhorn set her sights on wooing the great man, she waited for him to show at Sloppy Joe's. He did. And with that, the Key West chapters came to a close. By 1939, Hemingway and Gellhorn were Havana bound.

Hemingway Look-Alike Contest

ANDY NEWMAN—FLA-KEYS.COM

Every July, come rain, shine, or hurricane, Key West celebrates its great literary legend in its Hemingway Days festival. A three-day marlin tournament, a museum exhibition of memorabilia, literary readings, and a "Running of the Bulls" street fair also headline—as well as a short story writing contest. However, the undisputed highlight is the Hemingway Look-Alike Contest, naturally held at Sloppy Joe's on Duval, in which a parade of stocky, bearded contestants line the stage to compete for the honor. "Every man wants to write like Hemingway," according to one winner. Those who can't, settle for being mistaken for the great man in his prime.

Tennessee Williams Museum

Playwright Tennessee Williams arrived in Key West in 1941, after a play opening in Boston had flopped miserably. "Friday morning I was in Miami," he wrote to a friend back in New York, "and Saturday night I was in Sloppy Joe's in Key West. This is the most fantastic place that I have been yet in America. It is even more colorful than Frisco, New Orleans or Santa Fe." The "sights" impressed him. "The town is literally swarming with men in uniform, mostly sailors in very tight white pants . . . it is extremely interesting!"

MISSY JANES

On an early visit to Key West, Williams wrote a final draft of *A Streetcar Named Desire* at the La Concha Hotel. Like Hemingway, he was a relative unknown on his arrival. But he rose to international fame with the plays *The Glass Menagerie* and *Cat on a Hot Tin Roof* during his time on the island. Even after drink and pills encroached on his talent, Williams still rose every morning to churn out pages. He wrote *The Rose Tattoo* in his studio behind the modest little cottage he bought on Duncan Street, clacking away on his manual typewriter. Later he would insist on filming the movie adaptation in Key West. The Key West premiere of *The Rose Tattoo* was hosted by Williams at the San Carlos Institute.

Though he traveled frequently, the playwright always returned to Key West, his home and refuge until his death in 1983. His little Duncan Street house is closed to the public. But the Tennessee Williams Museum, maintained by the Key West Art & Historical Society, preserves the playwright's legend in photographs, first edition plays and books, videos—and even his typewriter.

To the world at large, Williams is remembered as one of this country's greatest playwrights, the recipient of two Pulitzer Prizes, Tony Awards, and the Presidential Medal of Freedom, among other honors. But to the LGBTQ community that would find a haven in Key West, Tennessee Williams was a forerunner and maverick.

MISSY JANES

Elizabeth Bishop House

The water "is the most beautiful clear pistachio color, ice-blue in the shade," wrote poet Elizabeth Bishop to a friend from Key West. A fishing fanatic, Bishop first visited Florida in 1936 with her partner, Louise Crane, winding up in Key West by Christmas time. They were guided through the waters by Eddie "Bra" Saunders, a Hemingway favorite, though by then the great man of letters was Havana bound.

Bishop was one of the phalanx of artists and writers who were drawn to Key West for its "natural pace," the booze, and rock-bottom prices of the Depression years—Wallace Stevens, Robert Frost, and John Dewey, among them. Bishop was just 25 and finding her way. Enraptured by Florida, she marveled at the soaring birds, the lizards scurrying underfoot, and the mangoes and guavas ripening on the trees. "I hope it will be my permanent home someday," she wrote. By 1938, she owned 625 White Street, a modest 1890s-era eyebrow house, whose "lines" she considered "to be the most elegant."

Bishop was a poet of "stunning gifts," though just as famously "self-absorbed, alcoholic, and lesbian." Her poetic style underwent a significant and lasting transformation, it's reported, during her years on White Street. Her first collection, *North and South*, published in 1946, was in large part devoted to Florida, the state with "the prettiest name," with many poems about Key West. A short time later, she would be anointed the U.S. Poet Laureate, and win a National Book Award and a Pulitzer, among a host of prizes.

In 2019 the White Street house was bought by the Key West Literary Seminar, an organization devoted to Key West's literary heritage. The house, open to the public, has been restored according to Bishop's copious notes and serves as the Seminar's headquarters.

ELLEN T. WHITE

Waterfront Playhouse

"When the sun sets, the curtain rises," they like to say at the Waterfront Playhouse on Mallory Square. As good as their word, the Playhouse produces an annual season of musicals, plays, and cabarets—undaunted even by staging full-blown Broadway blockbusters. It all began in 1939, when someone cried, "Hey, let's put on a show!" Banding together as the Key West Players, locals and Navy personnel performed, well, anywhere—on the decks of the U.S.S. *Gilmore* when there was no room on the island.

With the help of Tennessee Williams, a fellow Player, the troupe found a crumbling ice house on Mallory Square, once owned by Asa Tift, a notorious wrecker. In 1960, they converted it into a modern theater with 150 seats, which are now rarely empty in high season. The Waterfront is considered the oldest continuously running theater group in Florida. And while professional Equity actors usually headline, anyone can audition for a supporting role. All you need is to polish up a song and a soliloquy.

MISSY JANES

Red Barn Theatre

At a Red Barn Theatre performance, you are right there with the running water, what's cooking on the stove, or the fire crackling in the fireplace. The Red Barn says "big things in a small space"—the 88-seat house is, indeed, intimate. The building was the former carriage house to the 1829 mansion that fronts it on Duval (The Women's Club and a Curry Mansion). In the decades since world War II, various performance groups have taken it over. But it is the spirited group of actors and technicians that renovated the theater in 1980 that made the Red Barn Theatre what it is today.

Forty+ years later, from season to season, those same folks (and their children!) churn out what is generally agreed to be "Broadway-caliber plays"—occasionally consorting with big-name players. Richard Wilbur, the former U.S. Poet Laureate, produced his *Molière* translations with the Red Barn. Author Shel Silverstein gave the company carte blanche to put up his plays. Jimmy Buffett, Philip Burton, Terrence McNally, Jerry Herman, and Tennessee Williams have all consorted with the Red Barn during their time in Key West.

ELLEN T. WHITE

The Studios of Key West

"On that island, I found myself inspired not only by the ghosts of Ernest Hemingway, Tennessee Williams and Elizabeth Bishop, whose presences still lurk in many corners," wrote an early Studio resident, "but also by the vibrant community of writers and artists who live there now."

ELLEN T. WHITE

ELLEN T. WHITE

Hugh's View on the roof of the Studios provides a panorama of Key West and doubles as a performance space. JOHNNY WHITE

The Studios of Key West hosts artists from around the world in residencies and connects them with local talent, providing spaces where they can create together. The idea riffs on the legendary artist colonies—such as Yaddo and MacDowell—but with an important twist. At the Studios, the intent is to blur the line between artists and audience, letting everyone in on the creative process.

Pulitzer Prize winners, renowned artists, and celebrated musicians join local luminaries in creating a vast repertory of lectures, workshops, and partnership projects. The place bristles with creative energy. Performers might tackle a new playwright's work in a small black box theater. A veteran jazz musician might team up with a classicist for a rooftop concert. Studio galleries show the work of established and emerging artists, expanding ideas of art itself. Every day at the Studios, community members are taking the leap into writing their first short story or trying their hand at plein air painting.

From its Art Deco headquarters at the corner of Simonton and Eaton, the Studios has become the axis on which the Key West cultural community turns, causing a seismic shift in island values. Visitors who once headed to Key West in search of "sun and sin" now build vacations around workshops in memoir writing, stand-up comedy, design, or filmmaking. The renowned Books & Books, owned by author Judy Blume, stakes its claim on the ground floor.

MISSY JANES

The Tropic Cinema

It started with a few friends—movie buffs—who wanted more than Hollywood blockbusters from their film-going experience. So, in rental spaces around town, they screened indies, international favorites, and classics, inviting their friends along. Admittedly, the popcorn and Milk Duds were in short supply. In 2004, this growing club of film aficionados created a not-for-profit and opened the Tropic. You'll know it by its neon, Art Deco marquee—and, of course, the life-size sculpture of Marilyn Monroe standing outside.

The Tropic's four-screen multiplex is a throwback to a more glamorous era, when moviegoing meant plush seats and the popcorn butter was real. And audiences were focused on the screen ahead, not the one in their hands. In addition to a diverse selection of films from around the world, the Tropic hosts concerts and lectures, rolling out an actual red carpet for local and international premieres. Rachel McAdams, John Waters, Doug Liman, Mariel Hemingway, and authors Judy Blume and Meg Cabot are among the celebrities who have stepped inside.

Key West Handprint Fabrics: The Lilly Look

In 1961, three guys left the New York Broadway theater world behind and moved to Key West to open a silk-screen factory in a waterfront building. As luck would have it, they hired the fabulously talented island artist Suzie Zuzek dePoo to design their fabrics. Suzie's impish animal prints soon wowed designer Lilly Pulitzer, who defined a '60s silhouette —unstructured little shifts that society celebs like Jackie Kennedy wore from pool to party.

Under the banner of Key West Hand Print Fabrics, Suzie dePoo's designs catapulted the Lilly brand to fame and fortune. "The Lilly Look" was all the rage in resort wear in the '60s and '70s. At its height, Key West Hand Print Fabrics was the largest employer in Key West after the U.S. Navy. Lilly ultimately sold her brand and her interest in Hand Print Fabrics, but attributed her "phenomenal" success to Suzie's original designs and "whimsical creatures."

FLORIDA KEYS HISTORY CENTER—MONROE COUNTY LIBRARY

FLORIDA KEYS HISTORY CENTER—MONROE COUNTY LIBRARY

Gallery on Greene

Collector Nance Frank bought her first painting for $100 at 15 years old—a Fernando Botero oil—and later sold it for $30,000. So it comes as no surprise that she went into the business of art, opening Gallery on Greene in 1996. In the heart of the old seaport, the gallery is arguably the most highly curated, stylistically diverse in Key West, touting its connections to everyone from Tennessee Williams (who painted for relaxation) and the WPA artists (who literally painted the town in the '30s), to legends like Cuban-American folk artist Mario Sanchez, Key West idol Suzie dePoo, and the contemporary sensation Peter Vey.

Pulitzer Prize winners are among the group, and the work of a good half of the artists has landed in museum shows worldwide. Collectively the gallery's known and emerging artists capture the many facets of Key West in all its charm, madness, quirky history, and natural beauty. Some of the works are so sumptuously vivid, says Frank, you might be tempted to give them a lick. Do so, and you'll be taking them home.

MISSY JANES

Songwriters Festival

If Key West rivals Seattle and Austin as a music town, it is in no small part due to the annual Songwriters Festival, the largest gathering of its kind in the world. For five days each May, music lovers flock to the island to watch songwriters take the stage; many of them write for country greats such as Garth Brooks and Miranda Lambert. It's like being in Nashville's legendary Listening Room, some say, where mega hits are played by the writers themselves in the way they were intended.

It all started back in the last century at the Hog's Breath Saloon, where owner Charlie Bauer was booking live acts at the rate of three shows a day. A friend had a suggestion: How about a festival celebrating the writers chiseling away at songs in their garages? It started small. The first festival, held in 1995, featured six songwriters, including Shel Silverstein ("A Boy Named Sue") and Mickey Newbury. It evolved organically from sheer enthusiasm.

Decades later, in some 50 locations—bars, restaurants, docks, boats, and larger venues like the sparkling new Coffee Butler Amphitheater—hundreds of songwriters and singers now perform, from emerging talent to the hitmakers. The festival jump-started the careers of Kacey Musgraves, Florida Georgia Line, Jake Owen, Michael Ray, Randy Houser, and Maren Morris, and now straddles genres from country and Americana to pop and blues.

ROB O'NEAL—FLA-KEYS.COM

OUTPOSTS

Fort Zachary Taylor—Key West

The Gulf of Mexico swarmed with potential enemies, it was reported in the early 1840s, the Spanish and English among them. But this harrowing state of affairs wasn't addressed until Texas became a state, inflaming tensions with Mexico. To protect their interests, Congress approved funds to build a fort in Key West, begun in 1845. It was under construction five years later when President Zachary Taylor, a hero of the Mexican-American War, died in office. The huge, trapezoidal structure—impressively outfitted with a moat and a drawbridge—was named for the late president.

MISSY JANES

"Luckless" is often the word to describe Fort Zachary Taylor and its companion in the Dry Tortugas, Fort Jefferson, started a short time later. Hurricanes in 1846, 1850, and 1856 thwarted Fort Zach's construction schedule. Imported work crews were plagued by the heat; some made a run for it before tropical fevers caught up with them. Before it was finally completed in 1866, the fort was outdated. The rifled cannon, which shot a spinning cannonball into the masonry rather than bounce off it, rendered both brick fortresses obsolete. Yet the forts still had critical uses.

Before the outbreak of the Civil War, the Union Army held Fort Zach. As the only Union port south of the Mason-Dixon Line, Key West was instrumental in the blockade that squeezed the southern states. Within shooting distance of the fort, some 1,500 Confederate supply ships were detained in Key West harbor.

Fort Zach was again put to use during the Spanish-American War. Old artillery was buried when it was modernized. During restoration in the 1960s, many of those weapons were exhumed and remounted, giving Fort Zach the largest collection of Civil War cannon in the U.S.

Sand has filled in the moat surrounding the fort on the landward side, meaning that visitors can enter the fort on a dirt pathway. The man-made beaches nearby are considered the best in Key West. The surrounding park occupies a vast 87 acres where visitors frolic.

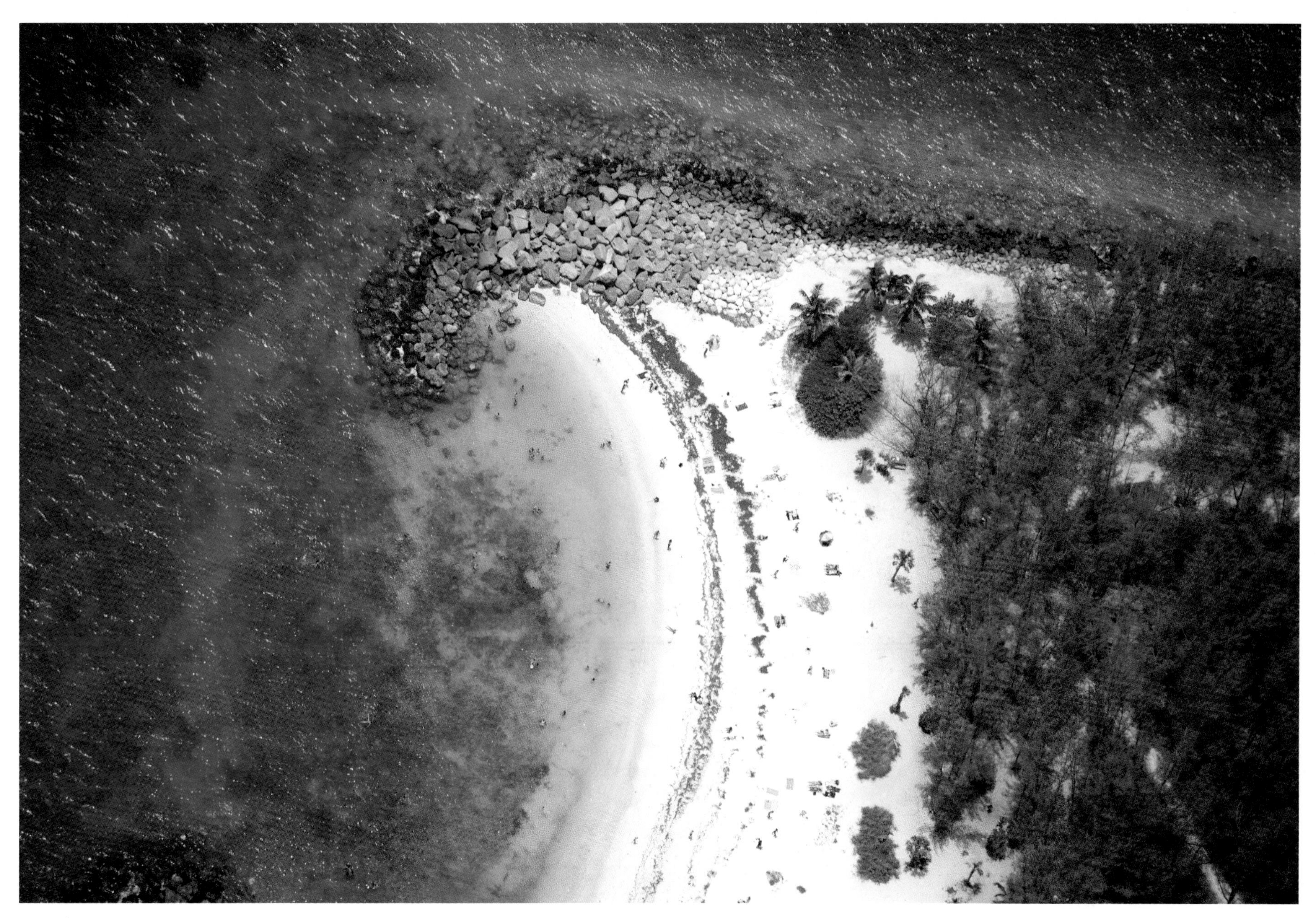

ROB O'NEAL—FLA-KEYS.COM

ANDY NEWMAN—FLA-KEYS.COM

Fort Jefferson—Dry Tortugas

In a not-so-terrible irony, no shot has ever been fired at an enemy from Fort Jefferson, the cutting edge in military architecture in its time. Begun in 1846, construction lingered over 30 years. Slaves provided the backbone of the work, as was true at Fort Zach; prisoners continued it. But Fort Jefferson was, in fact, outmoded long before the idea of its completion was shelved. Yet its strategic presence in the Dry Tortugas, 70 miles from Key West, poised on the all-important shipping lanes between the Gulf and the Atlantic, acted as a kind of fair warning to potential foes. The imposing hexagon remains the largest brick structure in the Western Hemisphere. Its ancient artillery—the Rodman cannons could shoot 300-pound shells for three miles—looks persuasively poised for action.

During the Civil War, Union warships used the harbor in their campaign to blockade shipping to the Confederate states. The fort was also a prison for Union deserters, worthy of mention for its most notorious inmate. Dr. Samuel Mudd set the broken leg of John Wilkes Booth, Lincoln's assassin, and failed to report it for 12 days, giving the fugitive a running advantage. Charged with seditious conspiracy, Mudd was imprisoned at Fort Jefferson in 1865. When the fort's doctor died in the yellow fever epidemic, Mudd took over, effectively redeeming himself. He served at Fort Jefferson for three years, seven months, and 12 days, and was pardoned on the final day of Andrew Jackson's presidency.

By 1874 Fort Jefferson was abandoned, but was later used as a coaling station. The U.S.S. *Maine* fueled there on its ill-fated trip to Havana, the event that ignited the Spanish-American War. In 1935, FDR turned Fort Jefferson into a national monument. The Dry Tortugas, including Fort Jefferson, has been a National Park since 1992, accessible only by boat or plane. The brick fort acts like a massive, nearly 16-acre reef; around its moat walls, coral grows and fish hang—making for good snorkeling. Visitors make the trek for the migrating birds, pristine beaches, silky waters, and endless sky.

ANNETTE HOLMSTROM

East and West Martello Towers

Are they forts? Historic sites? Abandoned buildings? Like so many other structures in Key West, the East and West Martello towers have led many lives, today having little to do with their original purpose.

The towers were started at the outbreak of the Civil War in 1862 to help Fort Zachary Taylor protect Key West, the improbable Union town, against Confederate invasion. As at Fort Zach and its doomed companion, Fort Jefferson, no shots were ever fired there in defense. Post war, however, bored soldiers stationed at Fort Zach practiced their aim on West Martello, reducing some of its brick work to rubble. Even in their apparent uselessness, the "martellos," or raised gun towers, are splendid examples of military architecture rare to North America, modeled as they were on defense towers on the Italian coast.

Nowadays, West Martello Tower is the home of the Key West Garden Club, a charming showcase for tropical flora. A visitor can easily wander inside, becoming an unwitting member of some private celebration by happy accident. But it is the East Martello Tower, nestled next to Key West Airport, that defies definition.

Once the headquarters of the Key West Art & Historical Society, Fort East Martello is just one of four historic sites under KWAHS's purview today. As a museum dedicated to the history of Key West, East Martello offers a delightfully haphazard and dusty take on the island's storied past—sponging, fishing, military exploits, the Cuban presence. But most people visit for the largest collection of haunted artifacts in Florida, including Robert the Doll, hands down the creepiest child's toy you're likely to encounter anywhere.

In the early 1900s, the doll was given to five-year-old Robert Eugene Otto and is a mini-me replica down to young Otto's sailor attire. Whenever Otto misbehaved, he blamed Robert the Doll, a habit that followed him into adulthood. Today, Robert the Doll apparently confounds visitors by changing his expression and mysteriously giggling. Dare to take a photo without asking Robert's permission, and bad luck will follow you out the door.

MISSY JANES

Behind the West Martello Tower is a Garden of Eden created by the Key West Garden Club, which is based in the fort. MISSY JANES

Robert the Doll is the creepiest child's toy you are likely to encounter anywhere. MISSY JANES

III

Proven Pleasures

If "One Human Family" were not the official motto of Key West, surely "Eat, Drink, and Be Merry" would be up for consideration. Since its earliest days, in the era of the wreckers, the island has been a place to cut loose. That attitude survives. A feeling of freedom that comes from being 100 miles from "civilization" persists, giving rise to a happy island of hedonists. Perhaps like no other vacation spot in the world, visitors give themselves permission to indulge—in great food, another round of drinks, that last toke that puts you over the line.

Of course, not every first timer to Key West feels obliged to participate in the famed "Duval Crawl," but many others pride themselves in repeating the experience once a year—and brag about it thereafter, in the grand tradition of Hemingway. Be forewarned that Key West is nothing like Vegas. What happens in Key West doesn't stay in Key West. No. It becomes the stuff of wedding toasts, family stories, even tombstone inscriptions down the line. Whether or not you're up for The Crawl, it would be a crying shame not to overindulge at Key West's brasseries. With the sea as a constant inspiration, dining is always a magical experience on the island.

THE DUVAL CRAWL & BEYOND

Sloppy Joe's

Sloppy Joe's is to Key West what Harry's Bar is to Paris—a place steeped in history and lore, fueled by the writers who hung there. Sloppy's was Ernest Hemingway's favorite Key West bar among many, where he brought his visiting "mob" of writer friends. When journalist Martha Gellhorn set her sights on the great man, she stalked him at Sloppy's. No fool Martha. Hemingway made Gellhorn his third wife.

Back in the day, Sloppy's was owned by Joe "Josie" Russell, Hemingway's fishing guide when he wasn't moonlighting as a bartender. Russell had a speakeasy over on Front Street during Prohibition. The two met when Russell cashed Hemingway's royalty check after the bank turned him down. In 1933, after the Volstead Act finally bit the dust and Prohibition ended, he had saved enough money to go legit. He took over The Blind Pig at 428 Greene Street, and briefly named it the Silver Slipper when a dance floor was added. But the place begged to be called Sloppy Joe's—Hemingway's nickname for Russell, as well as the name of a popular bar in Cuba with the same vibe.

In 1937, Russell's landlord raised the weekly rent on Sloppy's from $3 to $4. The incensed barkeep enlisted his patrons to move Sloppy's—lock, stock, and barrel—to a new place on Duval, where it remains today. Hemingway was Russell's silent partner in buying the building. When Hemingway dashed off to Cuba with his new wife, he stashed uncashed royalty checks, guns, hunting trophies, photographs, and original manuscripts, including sections of his Key West novel, *To Have and Have Not*, in Sloppy's back room, much of the stash only recently discovered. In place of old Sloppy's on Greene, you'll find another iconic saloon, Captain Tony's, which has its own colorful history.

KEY WEST LIBRARY

MISSY JANES

Captain Tony's Saloon

The building on Greene Street where you'll find Captain Tony's Saloon, built in 1851, has as checkered a history as Key West itself. It started as an icehouse that doubled as a city morgue—not a bad compromise on a tiny island. Toward the end of the century, it housed a wireless telegraph station, from which the sinking of the battleship *Maine* was announced to the world, touching off the Spanish-American War. When it became the Duval Club sometime later, owner Morgan Bird played host to lavish, "gay" parties until the military shut it down. Several speakeasies later, the joint was dubbed the Blind Pig. But to thirsty historians, its transformation into Sloppy Joe's bar in 1933 is the most significant occurrence.

The debate rages on—did Hemingway meet his third wife at Sloppy Joe's while it was still on Greene? Or later, when owner Joe Russell moved Sloppy's to Duval, in protest of a rent increase? You heard it here last: Hemingway met Martha Gellhorn in 1936, which puts the event squarely on Greene, as Sloppy's didn't relocate to Duval until 1938. Roulette, craps, blackjack, one-armed bandits, faro, and celo were the order of the day. Rumba was the music that patrons danced to all night.

Captain Tony Tarracino, the mayor of Key West for a short time, bought the bar in 1958. His saloon touts itself as the oldest bar in Key West—a fair call if you string together its past lives. But whether Jimmy Buffett got his start here is up for debate, as several watering holes in Key West claim the distinction. However, Buffett did immortalize the bar and Tarracino in his song "Last Mango in Paris."

The Saloon has changed little since the days of its late Captain Tony. The ceiling is covered with ladies' bras, the music plays on, and a pool hall has replaced the gambling tables. The bar stools are painted with the names of celebrity visitors, among them Ernest Hemingway, Truman Capote, Jimmy Buffett, Shel Silverstein, John Prine, John F. Kennedy, and Harry Truman. A more recent addition, Bob Dylan, who released the song "Key West (Philosopher Pirate)" in 2020, has frequented the saloon over the years.

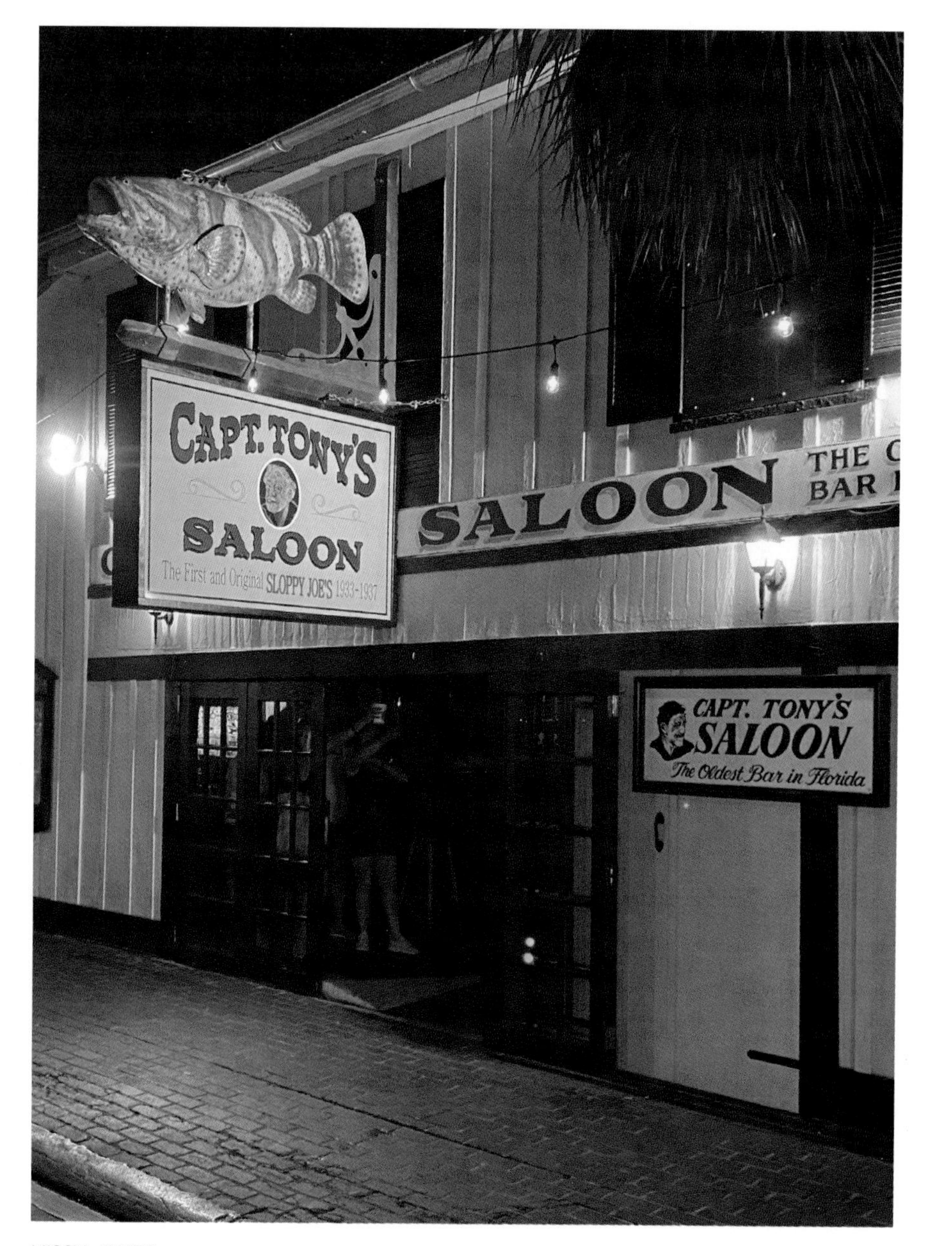

MISSY JANES

The Green Parrot

No place relishes its reputation as a dive bar more than The Green Parrot, where anything goes and "mind-blowing" bands play into the wee hours. "We are a jury of non-judging peers, a rugged and ragged council of friends," they proudly proclaim. "The Parrot has an engagingly louche clientele, a pool table and a dart board, odd art," says a local author, "and an attitude best described by the [misspelled] sign over the booze shelves: 'No Snivelling.'"

The Key West relic opened in 1890 as a Spanish grocery, owned by Anthony Sanchez—grandfather to Mario, the island's eternal artist laureate. Infectious Latin rhythms emanated from the grocery's small back room, where local musicians held impromptu descargas or jam sessions into the night. With the outbreak of World War II, the grocery became The Brown Derby Bar, a bunker-like hangout for submarine sailors stationed at the base a block away. So it continued until the 1970s, when then-owner Judy Sullivan turned it into the open-air hipster bar you see today.

The Parrot is routinely cited in the media as one of the best dive bars in the U.S., where "the management works tirelessly to avoid progress."

ANNETTE HOLMSTROM

MISSY JANES

The Smallest Bar

"Creative use of a broom closet," appreciative customers say of The Smallest Bar, or alternatively, "the size of a jail cell, though no orange jumpsuits required." Only Blomberg, Germany, offers a watering hole smaller than The Smallest Bar in Key West, which makes a virtue of its 72 square feet, permitting just two customers at a time. The joint is tucked away in Key West's old Custom House, which begat The Customs House Inn—currently operating as The Smallest Bar Inn, a resting place for overnight visitors who crave being at the center of the action. A bonafide destination, The Smallest Bar, a saloon known for creative cocktails offered at a price, is a time-honored stop on the Duval Crawl. Forward-thinking visitors book a room at the inn, so they won't have far to fall when they over-imbibe.

The Bull & Whistle Bar (and the Garden of Eden)

Actually, three bars in one, each on a separate floor, The Bull & Whistle accommodates all levels of inebriation. There is no way you can miss it at the corner of Caroline and Duval. Music emanates nightly in a tribal beat, and patrons spill out on the sidewalk, sometimes literally.

The 19th-century building first served as a boarding house and then a brothel, catering to the sailors and seamen passing through town. In the 1920s, during Prohibition, the place was a speakeasy, a gambling den, and a nifty smugglers' hideout, notorious even in Key West. In the 1950s, the building became a retail space, which it remained until the 1970s when a group of investors took it over.

The rowdy Bull on the first floor hosts local musicians. But it's the walls of the Bull's open-air space that will grab your attention. Murals depicting the history of Key West are all hand painted—Hemingway, Tennessee Williams, and Castro look on. From the more laid-back Whistle Bar on the second floor, you can take in the balcony view of Duval. But the night is young. With enough liquid courage, you could make it into the Garden of Eden on the roof, where clothing is, well, not required.

MISSY JANES

MISSY JANES

Hog's Breath Saloon

The Hog's Breath Saloon is the "brainchild" of Jerry Dorminy, an Alabama expatriate who left the mountains for Florida—though to call a bar a "brainchild," which they do, is a little like claiming your dog is a rocket scientist. The watering hole was first established in Ft. Walton Beach, Florida, in 1976, as a place where Dorminy and his friends could hang out together after a full day on the water sailing and fishing.

More than a decade later, Dorminy opened a second brainchild in Key West, across from Mallory Square with a prime view of the sunset. Its motto—"Hog's breath is better than no breath at all"—is a riff on his grandmother's maxim that "bad breath is better than no breath at all," a logic with which it's hard to argue. Yearly parties include a homemade bikini contest, the Hog's Breath Hog Trot, Hair of the Hog Leather and Lace party, and fishing tournaments including the famous Cobia Shootout. Don't ask.

Smokin' Tuna Saloon

Smokin' Tuna Saloon was built around live music—in fact the bar sponsors the Key West Songwriters Festival each May, in which hit-making songwriters perform their own songs in the way they imagined. But as dive bars go, Smokin' Tuna has a particularly civilized atmosphere, considering that it's just off Duval, a familiar stop on the Crawl. A picturesque old tree overhangs the secluded courtyard into which the saloon is quietly tucked away. The fairy lights strung into the beamed ceiling give the place a kind of tropical magic, enhanced by the craft beer when imbibed in quantity. Deep pockets are demanded at the raw bar; the fish is so fresh it might have just jumped out of the water.

MISSY JANES

The Chart Room

When the Pier House opened in 1968, patrons searched for the bar in vain. The Chart Room was not part of the original plan. However, with a few chairs and a mahogany bar, developer David Wolkowsky converted one of the hotel rooms into a tiny saloon, overnight. Wolkowsky had long been known for championing the writers, eccentrics, and artists who defined Key West culture. And while Jimmy Buffett technically got his start at Crazy Ophelia's nearby, it was at The Chart Room that he sang regularly, trying out his new material. His song "A Pirate Looks at 40" is widely thought to have been inspired by The Chart Room's bartender, Phil Clark.

While visitors routinely head for Sloppy Joe's, locals might be more commonly found at The Chart Room bar. Back in the day, the place attracted writers into its dimly lighted interior as surely as the promise of a Pulitzer Prize—among them were Truman Capote, Tennessee Williams, Hunter S. Thompson, Jim Harrison, Thomas McGuane, and Shel Silverstein. Local politicians once gathered there to plan the future of Key West over "lunch." Salvager Mel Fisher and his cohort plotted their way to finding the sunken *Atocha*, the 1622 Spanish galleon whose remains grace the Mel Fisher Museum. This is where Bob Marley is thought to have made his start.

Nothing has changed since the early days. That is, no sign has ever guided the uninitiated through the front door. Its walls and ceiling are still covered in faded dollar bills, aging maps, and celebrity photos. Popcorn, peanuts, and hot dogs are on offer just for showing up. There are no fancy drinks, unless you count the gin-laden Thirsty Pirate. No whirring blender noises.

So beloved is The Chart Room that some patrons never leave. Holes have been bored into the bar, and the ashes of several regulars have been spooned in and capped. Small plaques identify Mel Fisher, Panama Peat, Whistle Pants, and the mysterious Bob, about whom nobody knows anything. Because Florida law forbids disturbing human remains, The Chart Room is likely to stay just where it is for the foreseeable future. "The Chart Room is one of the last pieces of the soul of Key West," according to a local newspaper, perhaps quite literally.

MISSY JANES

ELLEN T. WHITE

The Speakeasy Inn/Rum Bar

Prohibition was a heady time for Key West, which essentially recognized the ban on liquor as an inconvenience on which to turn a profit. With Cuba just 90 miles away, rum-running became a viable sideline during the 1920s if your boat could make it through rough waters and ahead of the law. Speakeasies, which proliferated in Key West, offered illegal spirits to patrons on the sly.

A cigar selector by day, rumrunner Raul Vasquez turned his home at 1117 Duval—today The Speakeasy Inn—into a popular bar. Even without a sign, you couldn't have missed it. Vasquez had balcony woodwork cut in Cuba into an ingenious pattern of spirit bottles, hearts, diamonds, clubs, and spades, which signaled the good times to be found inside. A century later, that woodwork remains in pristine condition at The Speakeasy Inn, a legacy of Key West's wilder times.

Vasquez was finally captured by Prohibition agents and jailed for his clandestine activities—but he was allowed out during the day to take care of business. In the habit of returning late, he was given a duplicate key so that he could let himself in and out of jail at will. He would approve of the vast, entirely legal selection offered at the Speakeasy's Rum Bar today.

Schooner Wharf Bar

The bar used to serve drinks from aboard the schooner *Diamante* in the harbor but moved ashore, into the old Singleton Shrimp Factory. Soon, the place expanded into the building next door and added a second floor, the better to watch "the Sebago hustle away from its mooring as the Wolf returns to its berth after its sunset cruise," according to a patron.

If you are looking for seedy, you won't be disappointed here with this little piece of Key West history. "Nothing has changed much," says a repeat visitor, "except for a new screw or a board here and there." It was apparently a favorite of Mel Fisher, who called it "a treasure." The late Fisher, who famously found the Spanish galleon *Atocha* off the Dry Tortugas, should know what he was talking about.

On New Year's Eve, the Schooner Wharf Bar stages the popular "Lowering of the Pirate Wench," who happens to be the bar owner, Evalena Worthington, who with her husband was instrumental in restoring the historic harbor.

SUZANNE WADE

Aqua and 801 Bourbon Bar

Since the days of Tennessee Williams, Key West has celebrated queer culture entertainment, and nowhere is this more in evidence than in the nightclub scene on Duval. At both Aqua and 801, fabulously talented drag entertainers lip-synch to hit tunes, often coaxing their toe-tapping audience members into the limelight.

Local celebrities in their own right, performers such as "Sushi" and "Faith" have spent years on the Key West stages, sharpening their impersonations. You've got to love a place (Aqua) that once called its adjacent eatery Backdoor Poke. Or that serves up karaoke (801) with a side of bingo. Sharp, raunchy, always fun, "Reality Is a Drag" must go on, come hell, high water, or hurricane.

MISSY JANES

La Te Da

Most of the restoration of historic Key West is attributed to the LGBT population, who bought and revived old properties and turned them into guest houses, restaurants, and shops in the '70s. Among those was the handsome La Te Da on Duval, today a hotel and restaurant with a couple of swanky bars. But La Te Da's draw is its cabaret shows, which feature live, drag entertainers who give startling impersonations of Liza and Bette. But how La Te Da came by its name is the real showstopper.

The house itself was built in 1892 by Teodoro Perez, a successful cigar manufacturer. Like many expatriates, Perez was an ardent supporter of Cuban independence from Spain, supplying revolutionaries with money and arms through the Cuban Convention. When the poet and journalist José Martí—the voice and the hero of the movement—visited Key West in May 1892, he was greeted at the dock by thousands of supporters. Martí made such a rousing speech from Perez's second-floor balcony on Duval that the balcony was dubbed "La Terraza de Marti" or "The Balcony of Marti"—later shortened to "La Te Da."

The poet and revolutionary José Martí speaking from the balcony of what is today La Te Da. KEY WEST LIBRARY

MISSY JANES

SUBLIME SUSTENANCE

Louie's Backyard

Louie Signorelli, a legendary cook, opened his back porch to his dining friends in 1971—they included Jimmy Buffett, a then unknown singer, who rented the apartment next door. There were five tables, 12 seats in all, and offerings in the "Conch spirit" were part of the limited menu.

Buffett drew other members of his "rat pack" to Louie's, among them writers Hunter S. Thompson, Thomas McGuane, and Jim Harrison. Musician Eric Clapton showed up hoping to meet Buffett, whom he heard was a regular. Later, Goldie Hawn ventured in, as did funny men Billy Murray, P.J. O'Rourke, Johnny Carson, and David Letterman. Prince Albert of Monaco brought his vast security detail.

In his 1974 song "Trying to Reason with Hurricane Season," Buffett memorialized Louie's in the lyrics, "sure could use a bloody Mary, so I stumbled over to Louie's Backyard," which turned into "the bar next door" in some versions. In live concerts Buffett paid tribute to Louie's, flashing a backdrop photo of the hammock next door where he wrote the song.

Today's upscaled Louie's could serve gruel and still pack in diners night after night. The secret to Louie's success is not the gourmet fare, however excellent. A stone's throw from the Southernmost Point, the restaurant offers an unparalleled view of the Atlantic from its cascading decks, built since Louie passed on.

ELLEN T. WHITE

MISSY JANES

Salute! On The Beach

If a mermaid were to lunch with a friend in Key West, she would probably choose Salute! On The Beach and skitter across the sand of Higgs Beach to order a cocktail. No restaurant embodies the laidback beach life more than Salute!, where diners are at one with the elements.

That isn't to say that Salute! doesn't take its Italian-Key West fusion menu seriously. From snapper to spaghetti, they've got it going on. They'll be unphased if you arrive in your string bikini from beach volleyball nearby, or with your drooling canine companion on your arm. "I brought my dog," wrote a diner, "and they gave him a bowl of water before they took my drink order!"

MISSY JANES

Blue Heaven

When Suann and Richard Hatch took over the dilapidated blue-shuttered building in Bahama Village in 1992, they were smitten with the building's louche history. During Prohibition, Keys' residents bought their spirits here. The courtyard offered cockfights, gambling, and Friday night boxing matches, refereed by Hemingway. You can still slide back the tiny doors on peepholes and peer into the rooms of the former bordello on the second floor, now a gallery.

The Hatches fired up the property's ancient range and began serving black beans, rice, and fish for lunch. Soon they expanded the menu, using Mom's church cookbook for inspiration. Dinner was added with the arrival of Richard's brother, a chef. But it's Blue Heaven's brunch fare that has patrons waiting for up to two hours to sit down.

At Blue Heaven, chickens and cats roam among al fresco diners, cooled by canopies of tropical foliage. Everywhere you look, improvised art—a leopard-spotted mannequin, a rooster graveyard, jolly-colored coconuts—meets the eye. "We'll be together forever at the Blue Heaven rendezvous," go the lyrics to Jimmy Buffett's tribute to a Keys' icon, released in 1999.

MISSY JANES

ELLEN T. WHITE

Pepe's Cafe & Steakhouse

Few restaurants can say they opened in 1909 when Teddy Roosevelt was still president. Pepe's is, in fact, the oldest eatery in the Florida Keys and the second oldest in the state of Florida. It started out on Duval, where Rick's Bar now stands, surviving two world wars and the Great Depression.

Truman was a regular, stopping for coffee, as were a phalanx of celebrities looking for the Florida home cooking the restaurant offered. "Steak smothered in pork chops," inspired by an Errol Flynn film, became a trademark special, particularly popular among fishermen looking for anything that didn't come out of the water.

Pepe's landed on Caroline Street in the 1950s, in the weathered gray shack with a faded sign you see today. The joint has long been prized for its kitsch, cozy booths, and friendly atmosphere. At Pepe's, the fish, oysters, and fruit juices are guaranteed fresh. The freezer only has room for the ice cream.

Café Solé

If the legendary Julia Child had opened a restaurant in Key West, something like Café Solé would have been the consequence. Chef/owner John Correa cut his chops, so to speak, at restaurants in France, where he headed after his year of culinary training. On opening Café Solé in 1995, Correa applied French techniques to fresh seafood and, voila!—mutton snapper in pesto and champagne, yellowtail in a beurre blanc of lobster, and hogfish with red pepper zabaglione. And then there are the traditional French standards. With its twinkling candlelight and serene garden setting, Café Solé conjures up the intimate romance of the countryside of France, while preserving Key West's hallowed unpretentiousness.

MISSY JANES

Cafe Marquesa

If there is such a thing as sophisticated Key West, Cafe Marquesa is where you're likely to find it. The Cafe is part of the Marquesa Hotel, a complex of exquisitely restored Victorian homes that spans over two blocks of historic Old Town. You'll find the Cafe in the hotel's original building at 600 Fleming, which was built as a home by James Haskins in 1884. Incredibly, the structure missed by just 20 feet the sweep of the catastrophic Great Fire of 1886. Haskins's daughter, who became a nun, willed the property to an order of Catholic nuns in New York, from which the current owners bought it in 1987. By then, it had become a seedy hotel, sorely in need of renovation.

On an island teeming with small guest houses and behemoth waterfront motels, the Marquesa is a true luxury destination—probably the only one of its kind in Key West. Its restaurant follows suit, seating just 50 people in a dimly lit interior, magnified by mirrors on most of the walls. The menu might feature rarities such as tea-smoked quail with micro greens in blood orange vinaigrette or duck sliders with Tetilla cheese and umami ketchup. But its "contemporary American" fare includes grilled meats and, naturally, fish fresh out of the water.

MISSY JANES

Margaritaville Cafe Key West

There is no doubt that Margaritaville is a state of mind, induced by Jimmy Buffett's breakout 1977 hit, "Wasting Away Again in Margaritaville." But, as most everyone knows, it's also an empire of stores, hotels, bars, restaurants, luxury resorts, casinos, water parks, and retirement villages . . . not to mention daiquiri makers, tequila, beer, chips, frozen shrimp, salsa, salad dressing, pickleball paddles, footwear, and a radio station.

It all began when a restaurant chain tried to trademark the name "Margaritaville" as a specialty drink. Buffett sued and began branding his name, opening T-shirt shops and restaurants on his own, including the Margaritaville Cafe in Key West in 1987. Thirty years later, Buffett's net worth was estimated at $550 million from all his businesses, album sales, and tours. It's hard now to believe it all began on the day in 1971 when Buffett, coming off a failed album, cruised through Key West, blowing out his flip flop, and searching aimlessly for his now-legendary lost shaker of salt.

Parrotheads, aka, the singer's die-hard fans, pride themselves on growing better, not up, which was Key West's mantra long before the songwriter set foot on the island. Margaritaville, of course, can be "somewhere between the Port of Indecision and Southwest of Disorder." But it's also on Duval, where the original Cafe still stands, churning out Cheeseburgers in Paradise and festive drinks such as Changes in Latitudes, Proper Getaway, Tsunami, and Tropical Thunder.

MISSY JANES

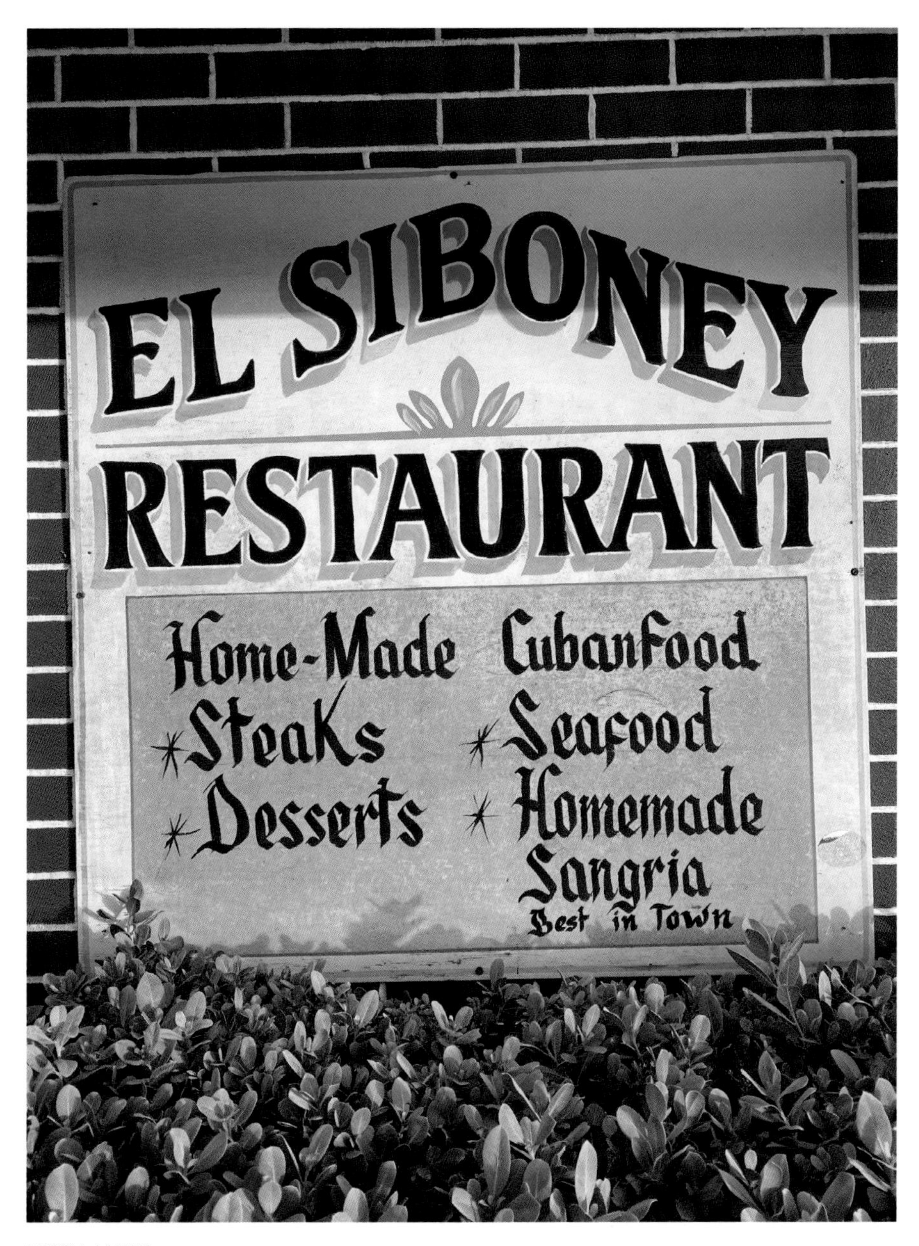

MISSY JANES

El Siboney

You can't find Cuban food, probably even in Havana, that so consistently hits its mark—ironic, since its owners, the de la Cruz family, hail from the Dominican Republic. By the time the de la Cruzes bought El Siboney from a Cuban couple in 2004, the restaurant had been a fixture in Old Town for 20 years. The de la Cruzes kept the restaurant's name, which refers to one of Cuba's lost indigenous tribes, as well as the original recipes that came with the bargain. The secret to the restaurant's continued success? In truth, to change nothing at all.

The roast pork is "softer and even silkier than a traditional pernil," reported *New York Times* food guru Sam Sifton. In fact, in an annual poll, the restaurant has been crowned Key West's Best Cuban Restaurant every year since 1993. It has duplicated its success with a place on Stock Island.

MISSY JANES

Half Shell Raw Bar

Originally built as a shrimp warehouse on the harbor, the Half Shell Raw Bar was established as a restaurant in 1972, just as the Key West shrimp industry moved out to Stock Island. It offers a taste of old Key West, where you can order the catch of the day and swill it down with a frosty beer, belly up to the bar or at an old-fashioned picnic table—better still, at sunset. Fishermen unload seafood live into the Half Shell Raw Bar's fish market while you eat. Two hundred oysters—shucked right onto your plate—meet that fate at the Half Shell daily during happy hour alone.

Better Than Sex

Some years back, Dani Johnson was determined to seduce her new husband, Len—with a double-layer Oreo cream cake that took four hours to make. Who knew it would be the beginning of Better Than Sex, a restaurant that not only turns dessert into the main event but treats it as a wholly erotic experience? The name started out as a joke. But when the Johnsons opened a place in Key West in 2008, Better Than Sex just fit. Desserts such as Cookie Nookie Pie, Between My Red Velvet Sheets Cheesecake, and Kiss Me, Carolyn followed—as did, eventually, franchises across the country.

The experience is immersive. From its windowless exterior on Simonton Street, Better Than Sex looks like a place that's up to no good. Inside, its "speakeasy" vibe plays out through red walls, erotic photographs, dim lighting, low-hanging chandeliers, and booths for two to four people separated by "privacy curtains." When you are served up tortillas layered with a tart semi-sweet chocolate filling and fresh strawberries—Berry Bondage, by name—prepare to submit. Or take the experience home along with the restaurant's handmade almond and aphrodisiac-scented Romance candle and the Better Than Sex soundtrack, also available on Sirius. Regular customers join a Friends with Benefits program. The sexual allusions are seemingly endless.

MISSY JANES

MATT JACKSON

Cuban Coffee Queen

Where would Duval Crawlers be the morning after without a piping-hot cafe con leche to soothe the way? No worries. In Key West, Cuban coffee is never in short supply. Ana's, Sandy's, and Three Brothers also all offer the thick, sweet elixir all day. But if you want "to do stupid things faster," Cuban Coffee Queen promises to up your game.

MISSY JANES

IV

Passions & Pursuits

The wreckers were, of course, the first to thrive in Key West. Then it was the spongers, followed by the turtlers, the shrimpers, and always the fishermen. On a four-by-two-mile island, suspended out in the middle of nowhere, lives and fortunes were made—and, of course, lost. The sea provided and took bounty, often without mercy. Through hurricanes, tropical storms, and floods, a passion for the sea prevails among those who make Key West their home, as well as those for whom the island is just a plane ride away.

While the wreckers are long gone, Key West still has the appetite for sea and its adventures: the parasailing, the schooners, jet skis, and catamarans that trip out over cerulean waters you won't find anywhere else in the continental U.S. The hunt for trophy fish draws anglers from all over the world. Divers still report epic panoramas along coral reefs, among the largest in the world. Many still lust for the treasures of the deep and dive in search of galleons lying dormant on the ocean floor. Others want to do nothing more than ponder their navels, drink in hand. For those, Key West's golden beaches beckon.

GETTY IMAGES

TO THE SEA

Historic Key West Seaport

When he purchased Key West in 1822, John Simonton saw the potential for deep water harbor in the bight, or bend, on the island's northwest side. Within years of Key West's settlement, the so-called Key West Bight was a thriving customs port and an international center of trade based on the blueprint that Simonton and his partners envisioned early on.

Along with wrecking, turtling and sponging would gain momentum as lucrative industries in Key West in the 19th century. Tourists gathered in the Bight to watch hundreds of live turtles—to be turned into steaks and soup—unloaded into "kraals." A century later, shrimp were discovered, resulting in the romantically named "Pink Gold Rush." Key West Bight would again change, pivot, and accommodate with new piers, warehouses, and processing plants. Fishing charters, even today, launch from the Bight in search of trophy fish or just dinner.

In January 1999, the Bight was officially renamed Key West Historic Seaport and Harborwalk. The *Western Union,* a schooner built in 1939, and Florida's last surviving authentic working tall ship, dominates the skyline. Two hundred years after its founding, the Historic Seaport remains a bustling port and the symbolic heart of Key West, as well as a destination for the most popular bars, restaurants, shops, and hotels on the island.

Key=West.

GETTY IMAGES—WOOD ENGRAVING 1899

MISSY JANES

Charter Boat Row

In 1876, at least one Key West sloop captain offered fishing charter services for a quaint $4.00 a day. But the pursuit of "fighting fish" in deep Key West waters—notably, tuna, swordfish, sailfish, marlin, and dolphin—wasn't "a thing" until the early 20th century, when Flagler's railroad opened up a steady stream of visitors to the island city. Serious anglers often hired experienced local captains to show them the way. Begly Filer, Luther Pinder, and Eddie "Bra" Saunders can all lay claim to being the "first." Saunders became part of Hemingway's "mob," assuring his place in Key West history.

The idea of Charter Boat Row grew out of the waterfront's piers and docks, where captains tied their boats and awaited anglers. Key West's Garrison Bight, a sheltered basin that was created from fill across its northern margin, became the hot spot for charter captains in the late '40s—for good reason. With their boats parked along the Bight's seawall fronting North Roosevelt Boulevard, captains could display their catch to motorists passing by. By the late 1960s, this was creating a public safety hazard.

In the 1970s, Charter Boat Row migrated to Garrison Bight's marina, where you see it today, flourishing as a mecca for fishermen from around the world. The imposing boats, with lofty "tuna towers," are typically 40 to 50 feet long. Salt water runs in the veins of Key West's captains, who will stop at nothing to keep the island's legend alive.

Ernest Hemingway on his boat Pilar with his favorite guide Josie Russell, also the proprietor of the famed Sloppy Joe's.
FLORIDA KEYS HISTORY CENTER—MONROE COUNTRY LIBRARY

"Flats Fishing"

While many fishermen pursue their game in the deep, others take it inshore, casting directly to fish they spy on the "flats" in shallow water. Inshore anglers might wade from the beach looking for quarry. Or they cast from skiffs or motorboats designed for the flats, which skim through the mangroves on the surface of the water.

As inshore fishing is practiced today, captains stand on a platform in the stern and use a "push pole" to propel the boat forward across the flat from the ocean floor; the angler prepares to cast from the bow. Stealth is the operative word here. The technique—developed in the 1940s in Florida and the Bahamas—cuts the motor. To increase the challenge, anglers often use flyrods with hand-tied "flies" that simulate bait. Typically, the sport is in the hunt. Once caught and reeled in, fish are released back into the water.

BRENDAN MCCARTHY

The wily permit is arguably the most difficult fish to catch on a fly. BRENDAN MCCARTHY

PAT FORD PHOTOS

Snapper, grouper, and snook are among the fish sought in Key West's inshore waters. But many anglers hope for bonefish, tarpon, and permit, winning bragging rights to a Grand Slam when all three are caught. Each species presents a special challenge. A 100-pound tarpon, Florida's signature fish, will put up a thrilling fight, leaping out of the water at the end of the line. Bonefish, "gray ghosts," are wily and hard to find. With their sharp vision, hearing, and powerful sense of smell, permit are the ultimate test. Anglers can go a lifetime without catching one on a fly.

Key West Bait & Tackle

You'll find the only bait and tackle shop in Key West right where you expect—on the Historic Seaport, steps from the water. At Key West Bait & Tackle, they can find you a guide who knows the waters. And even the novice fisherman can look the part with the shop's array of gear and apparel. But what good is your catch if you can't talk about it? Sympathetic anglers trade tales over icy cold beers at the shop's Live Bait Lounge, which specializes in chalkboard maxims such as, "Surround yourself with beer not negativity."

ELLEN T. WHITE

Coral Reef and Marine Sanctuary

Five miles off the Florida Keys, divers gravitate to the only living-coral barrier reef in North America, the third largest in the world. The reef teems with nearly 500 species of fish and 55 varieties of colorful coral. In good weather, the visibility through these clear, azure waters can be up to 80 feet. Professional dive photographers relocate to capture its wonders year-round. Novice and experienced divers go in search of bragging rights. A shipwreck trail of nine historic wrecks includes the S. S. *Vandenburg*, which, at 55 feet, is the second-largest ship intentionally sunk for the purpose of creating a reef.

So crucial is this reef to marine life of all kinds that the U.S. established the Florida Keys National Marine Sanctuary—some 300 nautical miles—to protect it. Yet global warming poses a constant and growing threat. Record-breaking temperatures of up to 101 degrees have bleached even the remedial efforts to restore it. By some estimates, nearly half the coral all over the world has been lost. Scientists do triage, planting coral. But with the main drivers of impact continuing to rise, efforts are only buying time until the problem can be solved.

GETTY IMAGES

GETTY IMAGES—STEPHEN FRINK

LOMBARDUWPHOTO.COM

Key West Beaches

The island may not have the expanse of beaches you'd find in Tahiti or Bora-Bora—no matter, Key Westers and visitors celebrate their intimate beauty with passionate fervor. In fact, they say that margaritas taste better on the beaches of Key West. It's because they are made with Key limes, delicately sweet, and Jimmy Buffett's lost shaker of salt, which turns up where you least expect it seaside.

Mostly man-made on the island of coral, the beaches extend from Fort Zachary Taylor at the southern tip in a gentle eastward swing along South Roosevelt Boulevard, where the Atlantic flows under the Overseas Highway. While you may never see Cuba just 90 miles away, even on a clear day, sunseekers are witness to some of the most spectacular sunsets on offer in tropical climes. From beaches like Higgs and Smathers, you can swim, snorkel, kayak, jet ski, parasail, and fish until you drop. In fact, many do, sometimes requiring the swift and sure intervention of the U.S. Coast Guard.

Each beach has its own personality, like Key Westers themselves, and their own unique history. Higgs Beach is the home of the African burial ground—the souls of rescued slaves graciously share the sun and sand with tireless volleyball players. On South Beach, a little ways from the

GETTY IMAGES—SNAP DECISION

MISSY JANES

Southernmost Hotel, a duel was fought on an October morning in 1829. Captain Hawkins succeeded only in wounding his lawyer, whom he had caught in bed with his wife. But he later "found satisfaction" when he shot his rival dead on Whitehead Street in broad daylight.

Dogs are allowed on Dog Beach, and to see them frolicking through the waves makes you wonder if they aren't actually amphibious creatures after all. There is no respite for the weary on Rest Beach. You'll be enrolled in yoga classes before you know it and meeting there every day at sunrise.

MISSY JANES

MISSY JANES

Key West Lighthouse and Keeper's Quarters

After the U.S. Navy established a base in Key West in 1823, a lighthouse was planned to help guide vessels safely through the treacherous waters of the Florida Keys. Michael Mabrity was appointed as keeper of the Key West Lighthouse on its completion in 1825. When Mabrity died nine years later, his wife, Barbara, took the helm, so to speak—a rarity in the 19th century. She would survive the Havana Hurricane of 1846, but not so the lighthouse itself. A Navy ship reported that "a white sand beach covers the spot where Key West Lighthouse stood." Fourteen souls who had sought refuge in the lighthouse were recovered nearby, including most of Mabrity's children.

A new lighthouse was constructed in 1848, built farther inland where you see it today. An undiminished Barbara Mabrity stepped up as its keeper. During the Civil War, however, she was fired, at age 84, for making remarks that were deemed disloyal to the Union. (Key West was under Union control during the Civil War.) Mabrity's descendants would serve as keepers of the lighthouse flame until 1915—which put it at some 70 years under the family's control. The Keeper's Quarters was completed in 1887.

After the Key West Lighthouse was electrified in the early 20th century, a full-time keeper was no longer needed. Advances in radar and sonar made the lighthouse itself obsolete by the 1960s. The Coast Guard decommissioned the Key West Lighthouse in 1969, after which it was turned over to the Key West Art & Historical Society. Today, it stands as a museum dedicated to Key West's maritime heritage. Visitors can walk up the 88 steps to the top of the lighthouse as well as explore the belongings, photographs, and diaries of the keepers and their families.

FLORIDA KEYS HISTORY CENTER—MONROE COUNTY LIBRARY

MISSY JANES

Key West Aquarium

At the height of the Depression, Key West was flat broke. The road to recovery was tied to plans to turn the island into a tourist destination. Under Roosevelt's Works Progress Administration, construction began on an Aquarium in 1933. With its "open air concept"—a first—sunlight illuminated the marine displays. Admission was a mere 15 cents, 5 cents for kids. In theory the Aquarium would not only draw thousands of visitors to Key West each year but become an invaluable resource for biologists worldwide.

Seven months after the Aquarium's grand opening in 1935, the Havana Hurricane bore down on the Middle Keys. The railroad—the only overland route to the Keys—was wiped out, along with dreams for the Aquarium. By 1943, the building was a military rifle range. But not for long. Leased back to the city in 1946, the Aquarium was restored to its former glory, more popular than when it opened in 1935.

In its 100,000 gallons of exhibitions, the Aquarium continues to tell the story of marine life in the waters of the Florida Keys and is actively involved in efforts to conserve its delicate ecosystem.

ELLEN T. WHITE

MISSY JANES

Key West Shipwreck Museum

Try to imagine Key West in, say, 1856, when swashbuckling "wreckers" ruled the island. According to legend, wreckers scanned the reefs from their vessels and observation towers, looking for signs of distress in the Florida Straits. The cry of "Wreck Ashore!" sent the town scrambling. The first to reach the sinking ship—aka, the master wrecker—controlled the cargo's salvage, taking up to 50 percent of the profits at public auction.

The Key West Shipwreck Museum puts you there with its observation tower offering a full view of the coral reefs and Key West's 100-square-block historic district. The museum itself re-creates a warehouse owned by the tycoon wrecker Asa Tift. Meet Tift himself—or, at least, his dramatic persona. Hear how wrecking enriched the entire island back when Key West was the largest and most cosmopolitan city in Florida.

The Shipwreck Museum's eye-popping artifacts come chiefly from the *Isaac Allerton*, which sank in 1856 on the Florida Keys reef. The water was so deep that salvage was a trial. Still, the wreck produced the largest monetary award the Federal Wrecking Court had ever recorded for a single vessel, the richest shipwreck in the history of the island. In 1985, the wreck was rediscovered, resulting in unimagined museum booty. The museum's relics also include those from Spanish galleons, such as the 1656 *Nuestra Senora de las Maravillas*.

Mel Fisher Maritime Museum

A flotilla of Spanish ships making their way through the Florida Straits in 1622 were swept off course by a hurricane. Galleons laden with "new world" treasure—notably, the *Nuestra Señora de Atocha* and the *Santa Margarita*—sank with a vast fortune in gold, silver, and precious stones. Frantic salvage operations began immediately. For the next two decades, the Spanish would fail to find the *Atocha* and the *Santa Margarita*. More than 300 years later, on Memorial Day 1985, a former Indiana chicken farmer named Mel Fisher pinpointed the $450 million mother lode after a 16-year search, inspiring treasure hunters the world over.

The Mel Fisher Maritime Museum marks the achievements of the man, who died in 1998, known for his persistent optimism—"Today's the day!" was his battle cry. Fisher's family shared his quest. Wife and business partner Deo Horton set a women's record by staying underwater for 50

FLORIDA KEYS HISTORY CENTER—MONROE COUNTY LIBRARY

MISSY JANES

hours. Tragically, his son Dirk, who found five bronze cannons from the *Atocha* as early as 1975, drowned with his wife when their bilge pump failed to operate. Fisher himself fought the State of Florida when it sought to coopt a substantial part of his fortune. The U.S. Supreme Court decided in his favor.

Many of the artifacts from Fisher's finds are displayed in the museum, including lavish treasures of gold and silver. And while much of its research and exhibitions are focused on shipwrecks from the colonial era, the museum isn't limited by subject or time. The goal is to explore man's ongoing relationship with the sea and the heroics of Key West's last true salvager.

Mel Fisher's RV *James Bay* working the *Atocha* wreck site FLORIDA KEYS HISTORY CENTER—MONROE COUNTY LIBRARY

Acknowledgments

After a day of fishing a few years back, Jed Lyons, CEO of the publishers Rowman & Littlefield, sauntered into Books & Books on Eaton Street in Key West and struck up a conversation with Emily Berg, the store's manager. "What book would you like to see on your shelves that you don't have now?" Jed reportedly asked. Never one to mince words, Emily had her answer ready, describing something close to the pages you now have in your hands. That night at dinner—at Louie's Backyard—my friend Jed asked me if I would be interested in taking on the project, which would become *Key West: Paradise Found*.

So, while I have Emily and Jed to thank for this dream assignment, there are many others whose guidance I couldn't have done without. Cori Convertito, PhD, Curator & Historian for the Key West Art & Historical Society, gave her invaluable advice and careful reading. Corey Malcom, PhD, Lead Historian in the Florida Keys History Center of the Monroe County Library, taught me how to search their photo database of historic images, created by the late Monroe County Historian Tom Hambright. So much of Florida Keys history would have slipped away if not for Tom's lifelong dedication. Over the years Richard Tamborrino, Chris Seymour, and Kevin Downey of *The Key West Citizen* have encouraged me to explore the Keys in articles that ranged from salt making and solar power to theater and maritime adventures, fostering the love I have for the islands now.

Photographer Missy Janes lived with us in Key West for six days while she moved from neighborhood to neighborhood, bringing her practiced eye to the Key West experience. Whiskey Rick Warmbold acted as her ready guide and my occasional fact checker. But I also thank friends and photographers Pat Ford, Michael and Suzanne Lombard, Brendan McCarthy, Andy Newman, Rob O'Neal, and Suzanne Wade, whose work appears within these pages.

I'd like to thank Paul Bresnick for his kindness and literary guidance, Barbara Bergeron for her eagle-eyed copy editing, and Lauren Younker, my early editor. Pineapple Press editor Debra Murphy has shepherded *Key West: Paradise Found* through various stages, always lending a ready ear, sage advice, and answers to obscure questions.

Forever and always, my thanks to Paul Dixon, my husband and champion. And to Robin, a steady companion by my side.

Among the many sources I consulted on Key West, I recommend these wonderful books: *Hidden History of the Florida Keys* by Laura

Albritton & Jerry Wilkinson (The History Press); *Key West in History* by Rodney and Loretta Carlisle (Pineapple Press); *The Houses of Key West* by Alex Caemmerer (Pineapple Press); *The History of Fishing in the Florida Keys: Angler's Paradise* by Bob T. Epstein (The History Press); *The Jews of Key West: Smugglers, Cigar Makers, and Revolutionaries* (1823-1969) by Arlo Haskell (Sand Paper Press); *The Ultimate Key West Travel Guide* by Mark Lee (Key Lime Press); *Mile Marker Zero: The Moveable Feast of Key West* by William McKeen (University Press of Florida); *Key West: History of an Island of Dreams* by Maureen Ogle (University Press of Florida); *The Florida Keys: A History of the Pioneers* by John Viele (Pineapple Press); *The Florida Keys: The Wreckers* by John Viele (Pineapple Press); and *The Florida Keys: A History & Guide* by Joy Williams (Random House).

For anyone who is planning a visit to the Keys, I recommend visiting the website fla-keys.com.

PAT FORD PHOTOS

MEMORIES

MEMORIES

GETTY IMAGES—LISA5201

GETTY IMAGES—CRAWFORD A. WILSON III

MEMORIES

MEMORIES

GETTY IMAGES—MATTEO COLOMBO

About the Author and Photographer

Ellen T. White is a freelance feature writer for newspapers and magazines—*The Key West Citizen*, among them—as well as, in years past, for a variety of cultural institutions such as the Carnegie Corporation, the Museum of Modern Art, and New York City Ballet. She is the former managing editor of The New York Public Library, where she launched *Bookmark*, their quarterly magazine. She is the author of *Simply Irresistible: Unleash Your Inner Siren and Mesmerize Men with Lessons from Some of the Most Famous and Infamous Women in History* (Running Press), a cheeky how-to that draws inspiration from the lives of the world's great romantic women, past and present. She serves on the Board of the Friends of the Key West Library, and lives with her husband Paul Dixon in Key West and on the East End of Long Island.

MISSY JANES

Missy Janes lives in Middleburg, Virginia just west of Washington, D.C. at the foot of the Blue Ridge Mountains. She photographs portraits of all kinds from farms and gardens through the seasons, to families and places near and far. She has carried a camera most of her life and began making prints for the local newspaper in the family dark room at age 12. Earlier books for this publisher include *A Walking Tour of the Georgetown Set* and *Palm Beach - The Essential Guide to America's Legendary Resort Town*.